Glimpses of Indian Heritage

Glimpses of Indian Heritage

RAMESH CHANDRA MISRA

INDIRA GANDHI RASHTRIYA MANAV SANGRAHALAYA
Bhopal (INDIA)

SERIALS PUBLICATIONS
New Delhi (INDIA)

Edition: 2011

ISBN: 978-81-8387-432-8

Published by
INDIRA GANDHI RASHTRIYA MANAV SANGRAHALAYA
Shamla Hills, Bhopal
(National Museum of Mankind)
&
SERIALS PUBLICATIONS
4830/24, Prahlad Street, Ansari Road
Darya Ganj, New Delhi-110002 (India)
Phone : 23245225. Fax : 91-11-23272135
E-mail: serials@sify.com

Contents

Foreword .... *vii*

Preface .... *ix*

1. Temples of North and South India 1

2. Ajanta and Bagh Paintings 54

3. Sculptures of Kushana Period 78

4. Two Islamic Monuments in Delhi and Agra 102

Foreword

It gives me immense pleasure in presenting this book on Glimpses of Indian cultural heritage by Shri Ramesh Chandra Misra, IAS, to our readers. Its co-publication by the Indira Gandhi Rashtriya Manav Sangrahalaya goes well with the mandates of the Museum to popularizing India's rich cultural heritage of art, sculpture and architecture.

The book is divided into four sections: temples, paintings, sculptures and architecture. Although the coverage of these sections is limited to a few familiar case studies, they certainly serve the purpose of arousing a sense of recollection of the wonder that India was. For an inquisitive reader, the author has lucidly presented the glimpses of Khajuraho, Konark, Kailasanatha, and Brihadiswara temples; Ajanta and Bagh paintings; sculptures of the Kushana period; and the tombs of Humayun and I'timad-ud-Daula.

The main strength of the book lies in its scope and coverage. It covers the period from Buddhist cave paintings of the 4th Century B.C. to the Islamic architecture of the 16th and 17th Centuries A.D. Without being too ambitious by incorporating minute details of each of these items, the author has very judiciously chosen to limit himself to the real glimpses, instead of broaching into the vast arena of Indian heritage. I feel, the accounts included in the manuscript could be best used by the researchers for comparison between different art forms and architectural styles of different times. The other strength of the book is its meticulous use of language skill in presenting the glimpses of Indian heritage without burdening the reader with too lengthy historical narratives.

Although the author, in all his modesty, declares that the "book does not lay any claim to original research, or critical observation", I am sure that it is the product of his persuasive scholarship and deep commitment to the subject. I express my sincere gratitude to the author, Shri Ramesh Chandra Misra, IAS, for kindly agreeing to get this book published by the Indira Gandhi Rashtriya Manav Sangrahalaya. I am sure, the book will be of great help to the students and scholars in art and archaeology.

Bhopal
24 September 2010

K. K. Misra
Director, IGRMS

Preface

We Indians are heir to a five-thousand year old ancient heritage; and yet the knowledge of an average educated Indian about our supreme achievements of art, sculpture and architecture is woefully poor. One does not have to be a historian or archaeologist to gain some idea of our rich artistic traditions. This book does not lay any claim to original research, or critical observation. The essays contained in the book were written as a part of the assignment given to me, when I did a part time Art Appreciation Cource in the National Museum Institute. My interest in India's built heritage was aroused during my working as Additional Director General of Archaeological Survey of India during 2002-2006. I never acquired any deep knowledge of this rich and colourful subject. But I did develop a conviction that preservation of this unique heritage is not only a responsibility of the Government, but also the collective responsibility of all of us as a nation.

A collection of essays by a lay author on some randomly selected aspects of India's heritage of monuments is certainly not a work of any important artistic or historical significance. However, it is an effort arising out of a geniune interest and conviction which the reader may like to appreciate.

Shri V. N. Prabhakar, who was Deputy Superintending Archaeologist in the ASI Headquarters, and is at present, the Superintending Archaeologist in Aurangabad Circle, helped me in putting this book together. For the photographs used in this book, I place on record my gratitude to the National Museum and Archaeological Survey of India.

I dedicate this book to Archaeological Survey of India, which since the year 1861 has been putting up valiant efforts to protect, conserve and preserve the ancient built heritage of this country.

Author

1

Temples of North and South India

PART I
KHAJURAHO

The Chandellas were initially feudatories of the Imperial Pratiharas who gained ascendancy after the fall of the Vardana dynasty during the middle of the 7th century AD. The Chandellas were busy protecting their masters, the Pratiharas from the onslaught of the Rashtrakutas of Malkhed. Yasovarman, a powerful and valiant Chandella king was instrumental in repelling the attacks of both the Rashtrakutas from the south and Palas from the east. An inscription from Khajuraho dated in 954 AD mentions the construction of a temple by Yasovarman dedicated to Vishnu. This temple is now identified with the Lakshmana temple.

Yasovarman's son Dhanga (ca. 950-1002 AD) consolidated the Chandella kingdom, discarded the Pratihara supremacy and due to his conquests, his kingdom extended from Vidisha to Gwalior and from Varanasi to Narmada. He is credited to have built the Visvanatha and Parsvanatha temples at Khajuraho.

Ganda, the son of Dhanga succeeded him and is known to have constructed the Vaishnava temple, known as Jagadambi and the Sun temple, now known as Chitragupta. His son Vidyadhara (ca. 1017-1029 AD), was probably the greatest among the Chandella rulers and during his reign the kingdom reached its zenith. Apart from his victories over the contemporary rivals like the Kalachuris and the Paramaras, he is credited to have organised attacks to repel the onslaught of the marauding Mahmud of Ghazni, twice, in 1019 and 1022 AD. He was a great patron of art and architecture as his predecessors and constructed the Kandariya Mahadeva temple, the highest watermark of Chandella architecture at Khajuraho. The temple is undoubtedly the largest and grandest temple at Khajuraho.

After Vidyadhara, the Chandella power lost its ground because of rising powers of Kalachuris and the Muslim invaders. However, Khajuraho remained as a centre of temple activity and many temples like the Vamana, Adinatha, Javari, Chaturbhuja and Duladeo were added during the first half of the 1st century AD. Khajuraho finds mention in the records of Ibn Battuta, who makes a reference to the temples here in 1335 AD. He mentions Khajuraho as Kajarra and refers to a great pond, about a mile in length, near which are temples containing idols.

Architecture of the Khajuraho Temples

The temples at Khajuraho are mainly constructed of fine grained variety of sandstone (except the Chausath-Yogini, Brahma and Lalguan-Mahadeva temples which are constructed of granite, largely or partly) in various shades of buff, pink or pale yellow. The sandstone was quarried from the quarries of Panna on the east bank of Ken river. The temples belong to various religious affiliations like Saiva, Vaishnava and Jaina sects. The temples at Khajuraho also represent the culmination of temple building activities of central India. They have peculiar plan and elevation features, which are characteristic of Chandella architecture.

The Khajuraho temples are generally without an enclosure wall and are constructed over and at the centre of a high platform-terrace *(jagati)*. The terrace also provides an open circumambulatory around the temple and elevates it from the surroundings. The temples are generally oriented on the east-west axis and the various compartments of the temples, viz "*ardhamandapa* (entrance porch), *mandapa* (hall), *antarala* (vestibule) and *garbhagriha* (sanctum sanctorum) are interconnected internally as well as externally, thus making the structures a single, compact structure. The *mandapas* of the larger temples have lateral transepts with balconied windows. Balconied windows are also added at the rear and lateral transepts of the *garbhagriha* of larger temples, which also provided the needed light to the ambulatory passage around the sanctum; the latter is another additional feature on larger temples. The projected balconies have a low bench *(kakshasana)* and are supported by finely sculpted brackets and covered by a flat roof with sloping *chhajjas* (eaves).

The temples also have distinct elevation features when compared to other regional styles. The elevation consists of a high *adhishthana* consisting of a series of ornamental mouldings; *jhangha* or wall portion consisting of two or more bands of sculptural motifs; *prastara* or the superstructure which resembles miniature shrines (*urusringas*), often considered to be representing a mountain range (Kailasa or Meru). The superstructure is crowned by a finial *(kalasa)*. The individual components of the temple like the *mahamandapa*, *mandapa* and the *ardhamandapa* too have *sikharas* but of pyramidal shape. The *sikhara* of the *garbhagriha* is curvilinear in shape. The *sikharas* of the individual component of the temple have a progressive ascent culminating in the *sikhara* of the *garbhagriha*.

The temples usually have an ornate *makara-torana* at the entrance of the *ardhamandapa*. The interiors of the temples are also decorated with exuberance of sculptures, on the doorways, pillars, architraves and ceilings.

The Temple

The Kandariya Mahadeva temple is the largest and most elaborate temple at Khajuraho. The temple which enshrines a marble Sivalinga measures 30.5 metres in length and height and 20 metres in width, the temple is constructed over a raised platform known as *jagati* which is a prominent feature among the Chandella temples in Khajuraho.

The temple consists of the *mukhamandapa, mandapa, mahamandapa, antarala* and the *garbhagriha* on plan. The *mahamandapa* has transepts on the lateral sides. The *garbhagriha* is enclosed by an ambulatory passage which has transepts on the south, west and northern sides.

The temple, as mentioned above, rests on a high *jagati* which is nearly 3 metres in height here, and the mouldings of the *jagati* are preserved at the south-eastern corner. The jagati of the Kandariya Mahadeo also exhibits a peculiar feature in the form of projections on the lateral sides and the rear, corresponding to the projections of the transepts of the temple. The *adhishthana* rests on the *jagati* which has intricately carved friezes of sculptural bands. These bands consist of elephants and horses, warriors and hunters, acrobats and musicians, dancers and devotees and scenes including *mithuna* couples. The bands on the wall portion depict beautifully sculpted array of gods and goddesses, *mithunas* and *sura-sundaris* on projections and *vyalas* and *nagis* in recesses.

This temple is also credited for having two *makara-toranas* with exquisite carvings on them. On elevation, the temple can be divided into the *jagati, adhishthana, jhanga* (wall portion), *sikhara,* and the *stupi.* As described above, the *jagati* and the *adhishthana* have intricately decorated mouldings depicting various motifs and decorations.

The *jhanga* or the wall portion rests over the *adhishthana* and consists of three rows of sculptures of equal size. These three rows of sculptures are relieved by two series of mouldings. The transepts of the *mukhamandapa* project out as *kakshasana* on the south and north and over this are the balconied windows canopied by ribbed eaves.

The individual parts of the temple namely the *mukhamandapa, mandapa, mahamandapa* and *garbhagriha* have their respective *sikharas* over them. Each *sikhara* is the form of an ascending tier and it culminates at the highest *sikhara* over the *garbhagriha.* The *sikhara* over the *garbhagriha* is surrounded by miniature *sikharas* on all the four sides and also numerous minor *sikharas* at the corners resembling a tall peak dotted with many small peaks of hills all around. This represents an imposing view of the *sikhara* and from a distance a visitor is awed with the tremendous rise in the *vimana* surmounting the *garbhagriha.*

The tallest of the *sikharas* is of the *garbhagriha* which has 12 *bhumis* or levels indicated by 11 *bhumi-amalakas* of semicircular section.

The temple houses many prominent gods and goddesses of the Brahmanical faith. This includes the depiction of divinities on the niches of the *adhishthana* with ten-armed dancing Ganesa, twelve-armed dancing Chamunda, four-armed dancing Indrani, four-armed dancing Varahi with a boar's head, four-armed dancing Vaishnavi, three-headed and four-armed Kaumari. Also found are four-armed dancing Mahesvari, three-headed and four-armed dancing Brahmani, six-armed Virabhadra, etc.

The images of Siva and Parvati constitute a major theme in the iconographic depiction here. The image of Siva along with the minor deities is shown depicted on the various bands of the *jhangha* portion with different postures and attributes.

The interior of the Kandariya Mahadeva temple is more spacious when compared to other temples. The interior is also decorated with sculptures and lavishly carved. The ambulatory passage walls are also decorated in every nook and corner and various bands of gods and goddesses, divinities, adorn them. The sanctum, in particular is elaborately decorated. The sanctum is entered through four stepped moonstones *(chandrasila)*, each flanked by conch-shells in bold relief. The lintel and the door-jamb is also lavishly decorated, the *lalata-bhimbha* is a four-armed seated, Siva riding on a bull, flanked by Brahma on the right and Vishnu on the left ends. The door-jamb has nine divisions *(sakhas)*, the first one is of stencilled scrolls, second and sixth with dancing *apsaras*, third and fifth with *vyalas*, fourth one with *mithunas*, seventh one with stencilled scrolls. The eighth and' ninth are decorated with lotus petals and wavy scrolls in bold relief ending in a *naga* figure. The usual Ganga and Yamuna panel is shown at the bottom of the door-jamb.

The sanctum of the temple is a square cell (2.73 m wide) with a sandstone platform supporting a marble Siva-linga enshrined in the middle of the sanctum. The exterior of the sanctum wall is also highly decorated with sculptural friezes. The bands represent processional frieze of elephants, horses and men, and miscellaneous scenes including erotic scenes.

The outer *adhishthana* contains nine niches. The images of ten-armed dancing Ganesa, twelve-armed dancing Chamunda, four-armed dancing Indrani, four-armed dancing Varahi, four-armed dancing Vaishnavi, three-headed and four-armed Kaumari, four-armed dancing Mahesvari, three-headed and four-armed dancing Brahmani and sixarmed Virabhadra are found in these niches, each image in one. Three rows of erotic compositions occur on the south face of the *adhishthana* of the *antarala* portion.

Inside the *mahamandapa* are noticed a series of niches counting to 23 in number. These niches are decorated with images like six-headed, four-legged and twelve-armed Sadasiva, three-headed Brahma-Brahmani, Siva-Parvati, Siva-Parvati as Kalyanasundara-murti, standing image of Siva-Parvati, Brahma-Brahmani, four-armed headless Vishnu seated on an anthropomorphic Garuda with wings, eight-armed image of Narasimha, four-armed Harihara, standing image of headless four-armed *ardhanarisvara*, eight-armed Siva, threeheaded and four-armed Brahma, seated Siva-Parvati, Bhairava, four-armed Parvati, seated Siva-Parvati, eight-armed Bhairva. Some of the niches are now empty.

Other significant and important sculptural representations found in this temple are of three-headed and eight-armed image of Vishnu as Vaikuntha, four-armed Indra, four-armed Agni, sixteen-armed image of Siva as *andhakasurasamharamurti*, four-armed Yama, Kubera and his consort, four-armed and bull-headed Vasu, four-armed seated Vishnu on his vehicle Gardua, four-armed Nirriti, sixteen-armed image of Nataraja, four-armed standing Varuna, eight-armed dancing Siva, four-armed Yama, four-armed Vayu, sixteen-armed Siva as tripurantaka, four-armed Isana, four-armed Gajalakshmi, seated Lakshmi-Narayana, etc.

Iconographically, the sculptures of this temple are more slender and taller than in the other temples and show the richest variety of apsaras. The apsaras are depicted in various postures carved with utmost elegance and style.

Sculptural Art at Khajuraho

The sculptural art at Khajuraho depicted on the various parts of the temples exhibit the most stupendous example of one of the medieval schools of art in India. The sculptural art here stands apart from other parts of India in the sense of the true representations of sensual character of the human body and its multi-faceted charms. The art here also is distinguished from other forms in a way that it represents the human body with beautiful profiles, three-quarter profiles and back-views. In particular, the graceful and beautiful exposition of the women of the contemporary era is another landmark of the Khajuraho temples. The art vividly portrays various human moods through various gestures and flexions.

The development of art may also be traced through the various depictions here. While the Lakshmana and Parsvanatha temples exhibit the art style with a more classical flavour, the Visvanatha temple depicts sculptures with more proportionate human forms. The sculptures of the Khajuraho temple are more slender when compared to the examples from other temples. Also, on the development aspect of art, the depiction attains its maturity here. The sculptures are tall, slender and exhibit various postures, some often turning around with unusual writhing, and also even in highly-contorted postures.

The bold and succinct portrayal of the erotic sculptures is also another example of the distinct sculptural art here. The erotic sculptures of Khajuraho are a major attraction. The exact reasons for representation of these erotic sculptures on the walls of the Khajuraho temples are not known. There have been various theories put forth by different scholars for the reasons to exhibit sculptures in such postures. These sculptures are examples of some of the well-composed representations of art here. The sculptures are portrayed in the most vivid nature, with proportionate body forms and of extremely good quality. The representations of such huge sculptural forms also reflect in a way the contemporary social beliefs and patterns. The presence of such sculptures was also not a taboo, as these find place with exceedingly well represented forms, postures and attires.

Significance of the Sculptures

The sculptural representations on the Kandaria Mahadeo temple like those of the other temples from Khajuraho reflect the contemporary society, the various peoples, professions, dress and ornaments, musicians and dances, courtesans, army, pageantry and processions, amusements, etc. The army is represented by the infantry, cavalry and the elephants. The armies are also shown in a marching mode. However, the actual combat scenes are rare.

Inscriptions

The Kandariya Mahadeo temple has one inscription engraved vertically on the southern pilaster of the vestibule between the mandapa and the mahamandapa. The inscription is dated to the first quarter of the 11th century AD based on palaeographical grounds. The inscription mentions the donation of the pilaster by the *Varastris* on the occasion of the *Navasurasamagama.*

PART II
SUN TEMPLE, KONARK

Introduction

Konarak is a village located at a distance of 66 km from Bhubaneswar, the capital of Orissa and is famous for the Sun Temple, which marks the highest point of achievement in the temple construction of Kalinga order in Orissa. The Sun Temple, even in the ruined form presents a majestic appearance in the midst of a vast stretch of sand. The name is after the presiding deity Konarka, the meaning of which is Arka (Sun) of *kana* (corner). The European travellers called the main temple as 'Black Pagoda' while the Puri Temple was known as 'White Pagoda', probably due to the colour of these temples when viewed from a distance from the coast. The black colour of Sun Temple could be due to the accumulation of moss, lichen and other fungal growth which turned the surface of the temple into black colour.

The legends attribute the temple to the Puranic age, and references are found in the *Bhavishya* and *Samba Purana.* This tradition is carried forward in the *Kapila-Samhita,* the *Madala-panji* (chronicle of the Jagannatha temple of Puri) and the Prachi-mahatmya. The traditions attribute the construction of the temple to Samba, the son of Lord Krishna, who after a curse suffering from leprosy, did a severe penance for twelve years to get himself cured. Samba cured of his illness by the Sun god, decided to construct the temple, and took a holy dip in Chandrabhaga and discovered the image of god, which was fashioned out of Surya's body by Visvakarma. The tradition also attributes that

Samba installed this image in the temple built by him in Mitravana.

The unpublished manuscript of *Madala-panji* mentions that a temple of Konarka-deva was constructed by one Purandara-kesari of Kesari dynasty in the Arka-khsetra. The Ganga dynasty, succeeded the Kesaris and Narasimhaeva, the son of Anangabhima constructed a temple in front of the temple built by Purandara-kesari and installed the image in the new temple. Narasimhadeva constructed this new temple to relieve his father's sin by not fulfilling the promise made to the God of Puri to enlarge the temple. Even though the tradition attributed in the *Madala-panji* is not reliable, the ground evidence at Konarak indicates that the main temple is constructed in front of a smaller temple, which might mark the location of the temple constructed by Purandara-kesari. The copper plates of the successors of Ganga king Narasimhadeva (c. 1238-1264) too mention Narasimha as the builder of a *mahat-kutira* (great cottage) of Ushnarasmi (Surya) in the corner of Trikona (*Trikona-kone kutirakam-achikaradUshnarasmeh*). The identification of Purandara-kesari is also doubtful. Some scholars feel that Purandara kesari may be identifiable with Somavamsi Puranjaya (7th century AD), grandson of Udyotakesari and brother of Kama.

The reason for selection of this site is not known. The temple for Sun could have been constructed because he is believed to the healer of diseases and bestower of wishes from very early times. The temple became very much popular during later times and the Vaishnavite saint Chaitanya (1486-1533 AD) visited the temple. Abu'l Fazl also mentions the temple in his *A'in-i-Akbari.* Abu'l Fazl describes the temple in details, but not its destruction or state of preservation. It indicates that during that time the temple was in good condition and did not face any destruction. The *Madala-panji* also mentions that in 1628 AD the temple was visited by Maharaja Narasimhadeva, the third king of Bhoi dynasty of Khurda, when Bakhar Khan was ruling the suba of Orissa on behalf of Shah Jahan.

The Marathas during the 18th century removed the Arunastambha made of chlorite and placed it in front of the Puri temple. The exact cause of the collapse of the main sikhara is also not fully understood. Various speculations have been made and various causes have been attributed to its collapse, like the damage caused due to an earthquake, loose foundation and settlement and noncompletion of the temple itself. The last theory has been discarded by the scholars. Evidence for uneven settlement of plinth or sagging foundation is also not available and hence it is generally agreed that after the temple fell into disuse, the damage was caused gradually and slowly. The periodic structural repairs which were necessary could not be made after the desecration of the temple and hence the stone elements, particularly the massive *amalaka* and the *khapura* members could have created heavy load over the superstructure and caused the deterioration to advance rapidly. The fact that the decay and collapse were gradual is substantiated by A. Stirling, who visited the site in 1825 AD, and mentions that the temple still stands, even in 1848, and a corner of the *rekha sikhara* remained to a considerable height.

The standing corner of the tower was further recorded by James Fergusson in 1837 AD who estimates its height as 140 to 150 feet (nearly 45 m) and Kittoe in 1838 AD who estimates its height as 80 or 100 feet (ranging between 24 and 30 m). This solitary remnant of the main temple also fell in October 1848 due to a strong gale. The visit of Rajendralal Mitra in 1868 mentions it as only an "enormous mass of stones studded with a few peepal trees here and there".

Architecture of the Konarak Temple

The Konarak temple was conceived as a huge and colossal chariot drawn by a team of seven horses depicted in the galloping mode. The entire temple was planned in such a way that it is fitted with twelve pairs of exquisitely decorated stone wheels. The horses were conceived in such a way that the Sun God (Surya) himself drives this chariot, his place being inside the *garbhagriha*. The Konarak temple also marks the culmination of the temple building architecture in Orissa. The humble beginning made in temple building activities in the 7th century AD (Parasuramesvara Temple being a classic example) passed through a process of efflorescence (e.g. Lingaraj Temple in the 11th century AD and the Jagannath temple in the 12th century AD) and finally culminated in the Konarak Temple in the 13th century AD.

Apart from the depiction of the stone wheels and the caparisoned horses drawing the colossal chariot of Sun God, the Konarak Temple is a typical example of the Orissan temple architecture. The temple is not different from those of other regions. On plan, the temple consists of a *deul* (sanctum sanctorum or the sanctuary), *antarala*, *jagmohana* (porch or the *mahamandapa*) and a *bhoga-mandapa*, the latter being detached from the main temple complex as a separate unit, but along the same alignment with the main temple. The only variation from the other temples of Orissa that can be viewed here is that the temple proper stands on a huge platform, the sidewalls of the platform utilised for the depiction of the richly embellished stone chariots.

The *deul* is a typical *rekha deula* of the Orissan order marked by the curvilinear *sikhara*, which could have been originally marked with the typical *karma-amalakas*. The *jagmohana* (frontal porch, *mahamandapa)* is the typical *pidha deul* with receding *pidhas* resembling a pyramidal roof. Both the *rekha* and *pidha deuls* were crowned by *amalaka* and a *stupi*. The *rekha* and *pidha deuls* are square on plan inside, while the outside is a typical example of a *pancha-ratha* structure known as *rathas* or *pagas* in Orissan architecture. The central projection, also the most pronounced one is known as *raha paga*, while the middle one is *anuratha-paga* and the corner one is known as *kanika-paga*. Apart from these major projections, numerous other minor projections and recesses could also be discernible.

On elevation, both the *pidha* and *rekha deulas* are divided into the components namely, *pishta* (or *jangha*, the platform), *bada* (the wall portion, the vertical wall), *gandi* (the portion immediately above the *bada*, the 'the trunk portion of a body'; in a rekha deul it is curvilinear, while in a *pidha deul* it is pyramidal) and *mastaka* (the crowning element, 'head'; it consists of *beki* (neck), *amala, khapuri, kalasa)*. It is also easily discernible that there is no marked difference between the *pidha* and *rekha deuls* up to the top of the bada portion. The *bada* portion further consists of *pabhaga* (foot) which is composed of five broad mouldings, *tala jangha* (lower shin), *bandhana* (a set of mouldings which divides the *jangha* into two, namely the *tala* and *upara jangha)*, *upara jangha* (upper shin) and the veranda which is again a set of mouldings, the number may vary, here in the *pidha-deul* there are ten mouldings.

The *pidha-deul* as described above is in the form of a stepped pyramid with receding tiers of *pidhas*, arranged into three tiers, called as *potalas*. The *gandi* portion of the *pidha-deul* is preserved fairly at the

Konarak temple. However, the *gandi* portion of the *rekha-deul* and a large part of the *bada* had collapsed long ago. Even the extant, remains of the *rekha-deul* remind us of the typical superstructure it should have once had. The *bhoga-mandapa* as stated above is detached from the main temple structure. The *mandapa* is a pillared edifice, now open to the sky.

The stones are laid in ashlar masonry, the individual stones were carved and finished smoothly and hence the joints are less visible. These stones were placed on one another firmly due to their own weight supplemented by the use of iron dowels to hold them properly in their place.

The evidence indicates that three different kinds of stones were used in the temple construction. The stone type known as khondalite was used largely for the temple construction while the high quality chlorite was used for the doorjamb and some sculptures. The interior core of the temple and other structures were largely constructed using the laterite stones. The selection of khondalite which is a variety of garnetifeours felspathic gneiss that is prone to easy weathering and chemical alteration had been a major cause in the gradual disintegration of the temple. Most of the garnet composition is decomposed into a spongy mass of oxide which is further deteriorated by the saline winds and heavy rainfall witnessed in this region. Hence it is been an arduous task conserving this temple.

The Temple Complex

The temple complex consists of the Temple 1 (main temple complex), Temple 2 (Mayadevi Temple), Temple 3 (Vaishnava Temple) and many other subsidiary structures like the gateway, well, kitchen, enclosure wall, etc.

Main Temple Complex

As described above, the entire temple was conceived as a huge and colossal chariot drawn by seven horses (three on the northern side and four on the southern side) over twelve pairs of stone wheels. The twelve wheels may symbolise the twelve months of the year.

Immediately below the platform and the *bada* is noticed an *upana*, which is a ledge-like projection and treated with decorations in friezes. The friezes are decorated with various themes, and the most recurring one is the elephant. The elephant motif is in various attitudes-elephants in defile, uprooting trees and branches, consuming the uprooted ones, feeding the younger ones, giving birth, fondling the younger ones and mates, etc. The next motif which dominates the *upana* is the military marches and processions. The procession consists of elephants, cavalry and infantry. The hunting of animals is also another theme that is depicted in the *upana* portion. Very often the king himself is shown hunting a boar or a deer and rarely a lion. The other themes that can be noticed are of the caravan scenes, pulling of a long rope by athletes, armed prince on a horseback, etc. The depiction of giraffe on the south side of the upana is an interesting and noteworthy one.

The *bada* or the platform of the temple is also richly sculpted and decorated in various bands. The *bada* portion of the temple measures nearly 4 m in height. The lower portion of the *bada* is further sub-divided into several bands that are depicted with various motifs like lotus petals, beaded pendants, creeper in foils and flowers, leaves and different animals. The *bada* portion also consists of several upright slabs and in between these slabs are niches many of them decorated with beautifully sculpted *kanyas* (damsels) in various moods and attitudes. They are shown as wringing water from the wet hair, standing nearby a half-opened door, standing underneath a tree, holding a branch of a tree, caressing a pet bird, making toilet, simply in a standing pose, playing musical instruments, etc. The upright slabs, are also decorated with motifs like a rampant vyala (a leonine figure on an elephant), erotic and amorous figures, nagas or nagis, each with human bust, a multi-hooded canopy and the tail of a serpent coiling round a pillar, beautifully depicted kanyas, miscellaneous figures, etc.

The wheels as already stated above, shown along the northern and southern walls of the platform holding the *pidha* and *rekha deuls* are another specimen of exquisite and skilful decoration of the Orissan sculptural art. Each wheel consists of a central hub and sixteen spokes, out of which eight are broad and eight thin. The hub and spokes are intricately decorated and sculpted with various figures and motifs. The spokes of the wheels are also sculpted in such a way that they broaden at the centre like that of a diamond and are thinner at the ends. The spokes are minutely carved with motifs like scroll-work, floral motifs, creepers and foliate, beaded strings and stylised *chaitya* windows. The central portion of the spokes which resemble a diamond is also relieved with various deities like Isana, Isani, Surya, Vishnu and his incarnations, erotic and amorous figures, *kanyas* in various poses, a nobleman with a man standing with folded hands, a princely cavalier, man playing on cymbals, a boar hunting scene, elephant riders, hunting scenes, etc. The axle of the wheel also contain deities like a god with a goddess, Gajalakshmi, Krishna playing flute, *gopis* and cows, Narasimha, king on an elephant, etc.

The mouldings of the *pidha deul* are also richly decorated with various sculptures and motifs. The *bada* portion of the *pidha deul* consists of several mouldings known as *pabhaga*, lower *jangha*, bandana, upper *jangha* and veranda, which in turn are sub-divided into several minor mouldings and richly decorated. The depiction of beautifully sculpted *navagriha* panels is noticed on the architrave portion of the *pidha*. The *grihas* which are depicted include that of Surya (Sun), Chandra (Moon), Mangala (Mars), Budha (Mercury), Brihaspati (Jupiter), Sukra (Venus) and Sani (Saturn). The Rahu and Ketu are also depicted nearby.

Among the doorframes, the eastern one is well preserved and nearly complete. The northern doorframe is also partially preserved. These doorframes were carved out of the high quality chlorite stones. The doorframes are another excellent specimen of decorative art. The doorjamb is divided into eight divisions. The base of each facet or division consists of a sculptural motif, starting from the innermost, a demonish figure, standing naga, two kinnaras (half animal and half human), a female, a male and a man with cows. The remaining portion on the three faces of the jamb is decorated with low relief sculptural decorations like foliated leaves, double coil of a hooded naga couple, succession of miniature pavilions with *vajra-mundis* containing figures, a motif with frolicking boys shown on a meandering creeper, vertical series of dwarf pilasters, succession of pavilions with erotic or amorous figures and sapuria (a motif containing fruits resembling pineapples).

As mentioned above, the entire *gandi* with the upper portion of the *bada* of the *rekha deul* has collapsed long time ago. However, the curvilinear shape of the *sikhara* could be gleaned out from the extant remains. The evidence of *pabhaga*, lower *jangha*, *bandhana*, upper *jangha*, veranda, *gandi*, etc could be discernible here. The lower *jangha* had provision for the housing of *dikpalas*; three of them are at present placed in the Konarak Museum, namely, the Agni, Yama and Nirruti, while the sculpture of Isana is now preserved in the National Museum, New Delhi. Several sculptures that might have originally adorned the rekha deul were also found in a clearance operation in 1906-07. These sculptures consist of one of the Adityas, worship of Jagannatha, Mahishasuramardini and *linga*, a marriage scene, King Narasimha in the company of priestly figures, King Narasimha on a swing, King Narasimha practising archery and a teacher discoursing to his pupils.

The depiction of *parsva-devatas*, representing Surya could be seen on the lower *jangha* at the south, west and north *raha* portions. The depiction of Surya on the southern niche is over a saptaratha chariot drawn by seven horses; the charioteer Aruna is also depicted. The god Surya is shown depicted with all the paraphernalia including kinnaras, his four wives namely Rajni, Nikshubha, Chhaya and Suvarchasa. Usha and Pratyusha the two divinities are also shown who represent dispelling darkness by shooting arrows.

A modern flight of steps along the northern face of the niche containing the western *parsva-devata* leads into the sanctum sanctorum. The sanctum contains a richly and lavishly decorated chlorite stone platform which could have once supported the presiding deity of the temple. The pedestal was found empty when it was first cleared off the debris. The Madala-panji mentions that the image was removed to the precincts of the temple of Jagannatha.

The doorframe of the sanctum is also richly decorated as that of the eastern doorframe of the *pidha deul*. The porch has staircases on its three sides and once it was originally guarded by a pair of colossi, two lions, each rampant on a crouching elephant, on the east, and two elephants on the north and south.

To the front of the eastern staircase of the porch, once stood the free-standing chlorite pillar, the *dhvaja-stambha,* with Aruna, the charioteer of Surya as the crowning element. The Aruna-stambha could be seen now in front of the main gate of the Jagannatha temple at Puri.

Mayadevi Temple

The temple of Mayadevi is located to the southwest of the Temple 1 which consists of a sanctum and a porch on plan. A narrow. apron of khondolite stone is placed all around the temple complex. The temple was exposed from the sea sand during the first decade of the last century and since then associated with Mayadevi, popularly believed to be one of the wives of Surya. However, the evidence indicates that this temple could have belonged to Surya himself, as this temple is dated earlier to the main temple (Temple 1). The sanctum was again empty when the debris was cleared. The tradition attributes that the image, known as Ramachandi which is under worship in a temple nearly 8 km from Konarak originally belonged to this temple. The tradition also attributes that Ramachandi left Konarak stealthily when the Muslims under Kalapahad overran the temple.

Vaishnava Temple

This temple is located to the southwest of Temple 2 and was exposed in 1956. The temple faces east and consists of a sanctum and a porch on plan. The temple was constructed of large bricks, and covered with a plaster of lime and sand. The superstructure is missing from this temple.

'Mithuna' Sculptures

One of the most discussed aspects of the Konarak temple is the abundance of erotic sculptures on the temple wall. Many British commentators expressed shock and outrage at this open display of rampant eroticism on a temple wall. Lowell Thomas described Konarak as the "most beautiful" and at the same time "the most obscene building in the world". However, various explanations have been offered for these *"mithunas"*, but no single explanation has succeeded in resolving the mystery. Benjamin Rowland and Percy Brown asserted that there was at that point of time, a *mithuna* movement involving orgiastic rites holding a spell over a large section of the people. But this explanation appears to be unfounded. The sun worship at Konarak had nothing to do with such orgiastic practices. The profusion of erotic sculptures need not also imply that there was moral laxity of the *devadasis* employed in the temples, who were primarily concerned with service to the deity.

Of greater credibility is the explanation offered by A. K. Coomaraswamy who mentioned that the Indian sex-symbolism is 'sacramental' in its likeness to the union of the individual soul with the universal spirit. The representation of sexual union in sculptures according to Stella Kramrisch is regarded as a "symbol of Moksha", because the ecstasy in sexual love was compared to religious ecstasy derived in merging of the human soul with the ultimate reality. Coomaraswamy further described the erotic sculptures as symbolic of the illusory world of pleasure in contrast to the solemn character of the inner side of the sanctuary. The outside of the temple represents various activities that belong to the *samsara;* beyond that and within the temple is the image of God. The worshipper must overcome the world of pleasure to find this God.

K. C. Panigrahi, a historian of Orissa, believes that the obscene figures were in all probability meant to test the self-restraint of a visitor before he was entitled to reap the merits of his visit to God. Another explanation offered is that the erotic figures are inspired by Tantric rituals. A further explanation is that erotic sculptures are meant to ward off lightning and thunder. Although various such explanations are offered for the depiction of eroticism in the Konarak sculptures, Coomaraswamy's holistic explanation appears to be more authentic. He says that such a characteristic feature of the temple architecture in India could be thought of as a representation of the rightful place of 'voluptuous ecstasy' in life. The erotic sculptures of Konarak reflect the life and vitality of the times; they are the expressions of a happy people who took delight in the pursuit of pleasure. The total frankness, lack of guilt, and the expression of mutual enjoyment and zest expressed through these sculptures have been noted by Nihar Ranjan Ray and Abanindra Nath Tagore. Prof. K.S. Behera, a noted historian agrees with these explanations and accepts this as most credible in his latest book "Konarak, the Black Pagoda" published by the Publications Division of the Government of India.

A comparison between the erotic sculptures of the Khajuraho temples and the Konarak temple can be noted. At Khajuraho, the sculptures being independent of the flat base of the temple body, seem as though they have been applied on the temple surface, without any basic relationship with the temple walls. But at Konarak, as in the case of the other temples of Orissa, the figure sculptures look as if they have blossomed forth from the temple wall. This organic relationship between the sculpture and the walls of the temple, contribute, to a very considerable degree, to the vitality and liveliness of the Orissan sculptures.

Aspects of Conservation

Another interesting aspect of the Konarak temple complex is the collapse of the main temple. Some scholars even believe that the main temple was never completed. Percy Brown asserted that the temple collapsed even before its completion. This theory, is however, not believable. The erection of the temple was undoubtedly the greatest achievement of Narasimha I. This fact was repeatedly recorded in the copper plate charters of his successors. The reference to this temple in the records of the successors of Narasimha I clearly proves that the temple was completed and the latest known reference made in the Kenduli plates of Narasimha IV of the Saka year 1305 (1384 AD) shows that at that time the monument was in a perfect state of preservation and the presiding deity was under worship. There is an inscription datable to the 14th century, on the temple itself mentioning assignment of deities for rituals to various officials of the temple. This means that the temple was completed, and ceremonies connected with worship were started. This evidence comes out from many other texts. Abul-Fazl, the famous historian of Mughal Emperor Akbar's court (1556-1605 AD) in his Ain-i-Akbari gave an account of the temple of Konarak standing in great prosperity. The European sailors accounts also mentioned about the "Black Pagoda" and "Jaggarnut Pagoda".

However, in course of time the main temple has collapsed. Rajendra Lal Mitra while visiting the temple in 1868, and Hunter in 1870, have recorded eye witness accounts of the ruins. There is something mysterious about the collapse of the temple, when temples of similar dimensions built earlier at Puri and Bhubaneswar stand today without major decay. Some scholars believe that the reason was a natural catastrophe like lightning or an earthquake. James Fergusson was of the view that it was because of the marshy foundation which could not support the enormous mass. There is also a theory that Kalapahar, a Muslim invader who desecrated the Jagannath temple at Puri in 1568, also attacked the Konarak temple paving the way to the ruin of the temple.

The temple in any case was exposed to very adverse conditions of nature like nearness to the shore, heavy monsoon showers, growth of vegetation on the temple, and saline affect. The temple was never repaired or maintained since its construction. In 1929 a stone which was covered with moss and lichen was examined by P. Parija, a Botanist of international repute. There were 357 layers on the stone. Accepting that one rainy season was necessary for deposit of one layer, 357 years must have elapsed for the formation of 357 layers. So the monument must not have been looked after since the year 1573 AD. In view of the long years of neglect, the dilapidation of the temple might have happened in the course of a slow and gradual process.

During the British rules, steps were taken for conservation of the remaining part of the temple. To save the *jagmohan* from possible collapse, the four entrances were permanently closed, and the interior was filled with sand vertically from the top by drilling a hole and pouring sand through a funnel. This was started in 1901 and completed in 1904 under the supervision of Bishan Swarup, Executive Engineer.

The conservation of the remaining part of the Konarak temple is still a challenge before the Archaeological Survey of India which took charge of the temple in 1939. A.L. Basham has said, "If the world wishes Konarak to be preserved for posterity, action and expensive action such as a developing country cannot afford alone, must be taken soon".

In the year 1984, the Sun Temple at Konarak was inscribed as a World Heritage Site by the UNESCO, in due recognition of its "outstanding universal value", and its uniqueness as a heritage of the mankind.

PART III
KAILASANATHA TEMPLE, KANCHIPURAM

Introduction

The earliest evidence for a religious edifice in south India follows the pattern of rock-cut excavation by Emperor Asoka (c. 273-236 BC). This has not survived due to the perishable nature of the building materials. However, certain edifices associated with the Jaina faith are found near Sittannavasal, district Pudukottai in Tamil Nadu. The evidence for a permanent medium for the temple building activities could be obtained from the Buddhist structures from eastern Andhra and northern Karnataka. The evidence from Tamil Nadu is lacking during the early centuries of the Christian era, even though literary references speak of temples built for various divinities. The Buddhist monastery excavated at Kaveripumpattinam belonging to the 1st-2nd centuries AD is a solitary example for a religious edifice, built of burnt bricks.

The Pallavas (c. 6th-9th centuries AD) were originally feudatories of the Satavahanas who once ruled the entire peninsular India, with the initial capital at Pratishthana (modern Paithan, near Aurangabad in Maharashtra) and later from Dhanyakataka (modern Amaravati, district Guntur in Andhra Pradesh). The Pallavas were also contemporary to the Ikshvakus, who in turn were also feudatories to the Satavahanas. The Ikshvakus during the 2nd-3rd centuries gained ascendancy on the decline of the Satavahana power and ascertained independence. They established their capital at Vijayapuri (Nagarjunakonda, in Andhra Pradesh) and repelled all other contemporary dynastic attacks. The Pallavas were among them and they were repelled into the northern part of Tamil Nadu, which was roughly the *Tondaimandalam* of the ancient period. The Pallavas established their capital at Kanchipuram, which also finds mention in the Allahabad Pillar Inscription of the Gupta Emperor Samudragupta I of the 3rd century AD. Samudragupta mentions the submission of Vishnugopa of Kanchi during his *aswamedha* expedition.

The Pallavas gradually gained ascendancy and were also responsible for expelling the mysterious 'Kalabhras', who once put an end to the rule of the Chera, Chola and Pandya dynasties in the southern india. The Pallavas glorify themselves to have completely liberated the *tondaimandalam* area from the 'Kalabhras'. The Pallavas were contemporary to the Western Chalukyas of Badami and the Pandyas of Madurai. The Western Chalukyas of Badami were great builders and they adopted the rock-cut architecture of the Deccan in their region. They followed the numerous examples of the rock-cut *chaityas* and *viharas* of the western Maharashtra and carved out beautiful rock-cut temples for Brahmanical and Jaina faiths. Mangalesa. the western Chalukyan ruler chose the finely grained and horizontally stratified soft sandstone cliffs at Badami for the excavations. The Pallavas, who had contacts with the Chalukyan territory were probably impressed with the permanent religious embellishments and were also induced to try similar ventures in their territory.

The earliest among the Pallava kings to excavate a rock-cut temple is Mahendravarman I (c. 580-630 AD). In contrast to the soft sandstone rock medium of the Chalukyas, the Pallavas chose the very hard and close-grained granite rock mass at Mandagapattu to create the Lakshitayatana dedicated to Trimurti. This is also due to the availability of granite as the primary geological formation in the southern India. Apart from the earliest examples of rock excavation with hard granite as a medium during the period of the Mauryas with examples at Barabar, Nagarjuni and Sitamarhi hills, the Pallavas were the only other dynasty to have ventured to use granite again as a medium for rock excavations.

He caused to excavate a shrine for Brahma, Siva and Vishnu at Mandagapattu in Tamil Nadu and claims through his inscription that "this brick-less, timber-less, mortar-less, metal-less 'abode of Lakshita was caused to be made by King Vichitrachitta for Brahma, Siva and Vishnu". This inscription clearly indicates that temples utilising brick, timber, metal, and utilising mortar were being built prior to the construction of this temple at Mandagapattu. Mahendravarman purposefully mentions that the Mandagapattu example is devoid of metal, brick, timber and mortar to indicate its permanent nature and hence an important landmark in the temple building style in southern India. Mahendravarman excavated many more temples in the granite outcrops. They are Pancha Pandava cave temple at Pallavaram (now converted into a dargah), Rudravalisvaram or Cave Temple 2 at Mamandur, Kal mandapam at Kuranganilmuttam, Vasantesvara at Vallam, Mahendra Vishnugriha at Mahendravadi, Vishnu cave temple or Cave temple 1 at Mamandur, Satrumallesvaralaya at Dalavanur and the Avanibhajana Pallavesvaragriha cave temple at Siyamangalam all in Tamil Nadu.

His son and successor Narasimhavarman Mamalla (c. 630-668) followed the tradition and created many more rock-cut temples in and around Mamallapuram, the port city of Pallavas. Narasimhavarman also introduced many new elements into the already existing Mahendra style. The pillars and pilasters became more slender and taller, also flatter, with oblong section, departing from the Mahendra style pillars which are bulky and massive. The most famous creations during the Narasimhavarman period are the bas relief of the Arjuna's or Bhagiratha's penance, Pancha Pandava Rathas or the Five Rathas, Varaha Cave, Mahisamardini Cave, Trimurti Cave at Mamallapuram. The rock-cut building tradition also continued during the period of his successors, viz, Mahendravarman II (c. 668-672), Paramesvara I (c. 672-700) and Narasimhavarman II Rajasimha (c. 700-728).

The period of Rajasimha saw the introduction of structural temples and the rock-cut examples gradually lost their significance. The tradition of building structural temples could have commenced as there was restriction for excavating rock-cut temples at their available places only. Hence a rock-cut temple cannot be created at a desired location according to a pre-conceived design and size and largely depended upon the nature and size of the rocky outcrop. Rajasimha experimented various stones for the construction of the structural temples, as this new building scheme was introduced during his period. He used the blackish hard variety of leptinite in the Shore Temple, the hard reddish gneiss in the Mukundanayanar temple and the softer greyish-white granite in the Olakkannesvara temple all in Mamallapuram and the hard pinkish gneiss at Talagirisvara Temple of Panamalai. Rajasimha could have observed that the usage of such hard stones like granite, chiselling and modelling them into wonderful sculptures and architectural members was time consuming. Hence, he also resorted to the soft stone tradition and also utili sed the coarse, friable, local sandstone for temple construction in his capital city, Kanchipuram. It is also observed that even though he used this medium for speedy construction of the structural temples, he did not discard the hard granite blocks which were used for the crucial load bearing elements and other crucial places in the architecture.

The Kailasanatha temple at Kanchipuram is one of the best examples utilising such a medium.

The Temple

The Kailasanatha temple is a joint venture of NarasimhavarmanII, Rajasimha and his son Mahendra III. The temple faces east and is, square on plan up to the *griva*, from thence it is octagonal up to the *sikhara*. The sanctum is also square and is double walled. The outer face of the sanctum is relieved with offsets on all the four sides and four corners. These offsets have small niches and are incorporated on the wall portion of the main temple. The corner offsets are square and provided with small two-storeyed *vimanas*, square on plan with four sided *kuta-sikharas*. The offsets on the four sides are oblong on plan with a similar dvitala vimana of oblong plan, with sala *sikharas* on the south, north and west. The offset on the eastern side is also oblong on plan surmounted by a *sala* superstructure, but it also provides an entrance to the main temple, thus functioning as an *antarala* passage to the main sanctum.

The above-mentioned *kuta* and *sala sikharas* are very well incorporated into the overall decorative pattern of the *hara* scheme above the *prastara* of the outer wall of the temple. The cells of these offsets have various forms of Siva enshrined in them. The *vimanas* of these cells also have different orientations, those on the south-east, south, north and north-east face the eastern direction as that of the main shrine of the temple, while those on the south-west, west and north-west face the western direction.

The outer wall of the sanctum between the abutting vimanas and cells is relieved with profuse carvings of gods and goddesses. The walls of the cells and vimanas are also carved profusely with various motifs. The garbhagriha is square on plan with plain walls except the rear wall. The rear wall is relieved by a small niche and is carved with a Somaskanda panel (low relief of Siva, Parvati and Skanda or Karttikeya on Parvati's lap). On either side of the Somaskanda panel are shown the images of standing Brahma and Vishnu. The *garbhagriha* has also a huge basalt *linga*, which is fluted and sixteen faceted and polished. The shrines of the early phase of the Pallava temples of the Mahendra I period had only low relief Somaskanda panels for worship.

There are also evidences to indicate that prior to the sculpting of low relief Somaskanda panels; the same image was painted on the rear wall of the *garbhagriha*. During the later phase, i.e. probably from the Narasimha I period onwards, the carving of the low relief Somaskanda panel became a normal feature in the sanctum. The addition of *linga* at the centre of the *garbhagriha* started quite late, probably from the times of the Rajasimha and this became a regular feature thence upon.

The massive superstructure of the temple rests on the doublewalled sanctum and over the bridge of slabs spanning the tops of the two massive walls and additional buttressing of the *vimanas*. The superstructure of the Kailasanatha temple is one of the largest of the contemporary period. An usual *vimana* of a Dravidian temple has various storeys in receding tiers thus resembling more or less a pyramid. Each storey is relieved with *hara* elements like the *sala* (oblong or rectangular miniature cell with similar superstructure), *kuta* (square miniature cell with similar superstructure) and a *panjara* (apsidal miniature cell with corresponding superstructure) on all the four sides. The superstructure starts immediately over the *prastara* (entablature). The immediate storey above the prastara is devoid of the *panjara* decoration, while the storeys above the first *tala* have the *panjara* decorations. The third storey also has the usual *sala*, *kuta* and *panajara* elements while the fourth storey has only four nandis on the four corners at its top.

The outer wall of the sanctum also has pilasters at the intervening spaces of the abutting *vimanas* which have the typical rearing vyala bases, which is a peculiar feature of the Rajasimha period temples.

In front of this temple and within the prakara wall is noticed a multi-pillared oblong mandapa, longer on the north-south axis. The corner pillars of this mandapa have the usual rearing vyala bases while, the rest of the pillars are plain with square base and top while the intervening part is octagonal in section. The entire temple complex is enclosed by a prakara wall with a large opening on the east. The large opening on the east is occupied by a shrine having two-storeyed oblong vimana which can be very well gleaned from its appearance as the precursor of the later period tall and massive *gopuras* (entrance gateways) of the temple complexes. This shrine is known as the Mahendravarmesvara, named after the son of Rajasimha and consists of a sanctum and an *ardhamandapa*. The sanctum of this small shrine is relieved by the usual linga and the Somaskanda panel, the latter executed on its rear wall. The shrine is also relieved with the sculptures of Brahma and Vishnu in the *ardhamandapa* and several other gods and goddesses on the outer wall.

The enclosure wall of the entire temple complex also has an entrance on its west, which is surmounted by a *gopura*, with an oblong superstructure. This is a *gopura* in a real sense, and as mentioned above, along with the superstructure over the small shrine near the eastern shrine, represents the earliest form of the gopura entrances to the south Indian temples. The inner wall of the *prakara* is relieved with fifty-eight small shrines. All are square on plan except two which are oblong on plan. These shrines are dedicated to Siva except the oblong ones, which are located one each on the north and south and facing the main shrine. These two oblong shrines are dedicated to Vishnu (shrine facing south) and Brahma (shrine facing north). These small shrines exhibit various specimens of the Pallava mural paintings. These paintings could be observed both on the plain wall portions of the shrine as well as painted stucco over relief. At certain places, even today the original pigments of the Pallava painters could be seen. These paintings may belong to two different periods, while the paintings executed on the plaster over the sandstone surfaces belong to the Pallava period; there are also traces of plastering of the coarse sandstone surfaces during the later periods, which were also painted.

This is further substantiated by an inscription of the Chola Kulottunga I (c. 1070 AD) on a stone slab, which was ultimately plastered and paintings executed over them.

The external wall portions of the temples are at places relieved with various sculptural decorations. The themes are both Saivite and Vaishnavite on a variety of sculptures. Some of the sculptures include the Ganesa, Saptamatrika group, Chandesa, *parivara* deities, etc. The *dvarapalakas* also make a good representation of the Pallava sculptural art along with the above mentioned sculptures.

The inscriptions found on one of the pillars of the front *mandapa* of the temple speak of the conquest of Pallava territory by Vikramaditya I of the western Chalukyan dynasty, who captured the Pallava capital, Kanchipuram, as an act of retaliation to the conquest of Badami, the Chalukyan capital by Narasimhavarman. Vikramaditya claims that he did not destroy the Pallava capital and even endowed the temples with gifts and donations. He even took the architects and sculptors from the Pallava territory and constructed many temples in the Chalukyan territory. It is often said that the temples at Pattadakkal and Ellora are very much similar to the Kailasanatha Temple of Kanchipuram. Such is the grandiose nature of this temple that it left a great impression not only on the minds of the contemporary rulers of the Pallavas, but even after a gap of nearly 1300 years, it is still enchanting in its appearance. The temple also stands testimony as a major landmark in the temple building activity of southern India and a very good example of the transitional phase between the rock-cut and structural examples.

The Kailasanatha Temple fell into disuse during the later Chola period onwards until its revival during the Vijayanagara period. Prince Kampanna of the Vijayanagara dynasty is said to have repaired the temple and revived the worship. There are even traces of the paintings of the Vijayanagara period in this temple, which bear testimony of the efforts made by the members of the royal family of the Vijayanagara dynasty.

PART IV
BRIHADISWARA TEMPLE, THANJAVUR

Introduction

The Brihadiswara Temple or the *Periya Koyil* (Big Temple), as it is locally known, is a major landmark in the south Indian temple architecture. The temple is located in Thanjavur, the district headquarters of the same name in Tamil Nadu. Thanjavur is located at a distance of about 332 km southwest of Chennai.

The temple was built during the reign of the imperial Cholas who ruled the southern part of India from ninth to twelfth centuries. The imperial Cholas trace their ancestry to the Surya or the Raghuvansa. However, during the early part of the Christian era, the Sangam age Cholas ruled along with the Cheras and Pandyas in the southern part of India. The Cholas also find mention in the rock edicts of Emperor Asoka of the third century BC. Karikala, the famous early Chola emperor is famous for having united the entire kingdoms of the south and is also credited to have constructed a stone dam across the River Cauvery. After the third century AD. the Cholas lost their dominance and soon the Pallavas took over control of south India.

The Cholas again surface as the feudatories of the Pallavas during the 8th-9th century AD. It was in ca. 850 AD that Vijayala Chola established a small kingdom around Thanjavur, with its capital at Uraiyur. His son and grandson were Aditya Chola and Parantaka Chola who gradually established control over many parts of the southern India. They also were great temple builders and are credited with a number of structural temples, which marked a great deviation from the rock cut temples of the Pallavas. Parantaka was a prominent ruler of the imperial Cholas, who conquered the southern kingdom of Pandyas and also Sri Lanka and assumed the title *Maduraiyum Ilamumkonda* [one who conquered Madurai (seat of Pandyas) and Sri Lanka].

Rajaditya, the eldest son of Parantaka lost his life on an elephant during a war with the Rashtrakuta Krishna III. Hence his brother Gandaraditya ascended the throne, but he also soon lost his life and hence his brother Arinjaya became the king of the Cholas. Arinjaya also lost his life in a battlefield while fighting the Rashtrakutas to regain the lost territories during his predecessors. Arinjaya's son Sundara Chola succeeded to the throne and his eldest son Aditya was a great warrior and was the crown prince when he was assassinated. Arulmolivarman, the brother of Aditya Chola, refused to ascend the throne as his uncle Uttama Chola, the son of Gandaraditya was grown up. Arulmolivarman ultimately ascended the throne in 985 AD and assumed the title Rajaraja Chola.

Rajaraja Chola was probably the greatest ruler among the Chola emperors. He was a great conqueror, administrator, a great patron of art and architecture only to be surpassed by his son and successor Rajendra Chola. As soon as he ascended the throne, Rajaraja consolidated his throne by successively defeating the Keralas, Pandyas and Simhalas; Gangas, Chalukya Satyasraya. At first, he defeated the confederation of armies of the Keralas, Pandyas and the Simhalas. Later he pursued the Simhala king Mahinda V through a naval expedition and took control of the northern part of Sri Lanka and made Polannaruva as the capital of the Chola province. The Chalukya Satyasraya was repelled by the Chola army under his son Rajendra I, who captured Banavasi and a large part of Raichur Doab. He entered into matrimonial relationship with the eastern Chalukyan king by marrying his daughter Kundavai to Vimaladitya, the brother of Saktivarman the Chalukyan ruler. Rajendra, his son established a pillar of victory on the Mahendra hill in Kalinga. Rajaraja also captured the Maldive islands from the Chera control and established his sway over the islands adjoining Maldives. The Leyden grant of Rajaraja mentions that the Sailendra king of Sri Vijaya (Palembang) and Kataha (Kedah), Sri Mara

Vijayaottungavarman was allowed to construct a Buddhist vihara at Nagapattinam, named as Cudamani and Rajaraja granted a village of Anaimangalam for the vihara.

Rajaraja built the Brihadiswara temple which probably is the culmination of the vimana architecture of south India temples.

Endowments to the Temple

The numerous inscriptions on the walls of the temple reflect the status of religion, art, administration, etc., of the contemporary era. The inscription also mentions that the temple was provided with a golden finial by the Emperor Rajaraja during his 275th day of his 25th year of his reign (1010 AD). The temple is dedicated to Siva and Rajaraja named it as Rajarajesvaram-udaiyar after himself.

Rajaraja caused several endowments to the temple for its maintenance. He was joined by his family members and other high officials from his government in donating various endowments to the temple. The inscriptions list several bronze and gold images, ornaments for decorating these images, etc. Most of the exquisite representations of the Chola art have been lost, but a handful of them are still to be seen in the form of Nataraja, Tripurantaka, Devi and Ganesa. The endowments of Rajaraja and his kith and kin are detailed in respect of even the smallest weights and measures, the methodology of receiving, the payment details, interest rates, conduct of worship of special items, provision of perpetual burning of lamps, etc are mentioned in the inscriptions. The endowments were so skilfully planned that even provisions for the cooks, gardeners, flowergatherers, garland makers, musicians, drummers, dancers, dance masters, wood carvers, sculptors, painters, choir-groups for singing hymns in Sanskrit and Tamil, accountants, watchmen, host of other officials and servants for the temple were made and find mention in the inscriptions. Rajaraja even caused two long streets for housing nearly four hundred women dancers attached to the temple.

These are the best sources to know about the contemporary history, customs and practices, organisation of society, etc. The temples were the centres of great political and social activity during those times and were the centres of art, culture, religion, dance and music. Even administrative cases were decided in the temple premises.

No wonder that Rajaraja after his assuming charge of the entire southern India should have decided to establish an even more perpetual icon of his superiority in the form of this great temple.

General Features of a Chola Temple (Dravidian Style)

The two major temple styles of ancient India, namely the Nagara and Dravida, was formalised and crystallised during the fifth and sixth centuries AD. The Dravidian style of construction was initiated largely by the Pallavas in a more permanent medium during the sixth century AD which reached its culmination under the Cholas.

The development of this style could be discernible from the examples at Mahabalipuram and Kanchipuram which were the major Pallava centres of art and commerce. The Kailasanatha temple at Kanchipuram is an example of a complete temple complex, consisting of a *garbhagriha, antarala, mandapa* enclosed by a cloistered enclosure wall with an entrance *gopura.* The *sikhara* of a Dravidian temple is square on plan and pyramidal on elevation unlike that, of a Nagara temple which is square on plan and curvilinear on elevation. The *sikhara* is divided into various tiers or storeys by the arrangement of miniature shrines of three types, namely, the *sala* (rectangular), *kuta* (square) and *panjara* (apsidal). The arrangement of the pillar elements is improvised from their Pallava examples in terms of elaboration and additional elements. The Dravidian order of temples attained its zenith under the Cholas and ultimately under Rajaraja I, which is reflected in the Brihadisvara Temple.

The main shrine is the most dominant feature of the Chola temples, and in the Brihadisvara temple, it reaches the highest watermark. The *sikhara* of the Brihadisvara temple is the tallest among all the temples of south India. The construction of the entrance *gopura* also crystallises during this period which is reflected in the first entrance *gopura* of the temple.

The Temple

The temple complex is surrounded by a moat on the west, north and east, the Grant Anicut Canal on its south. The temple is constructed entirely of granite, like many other temples in south India. However, the Thanjavur area is devoid of this type of stone as it is an alluvium of the River Cauvery. Hence the granite for this temple construction was quarried and transported from a long distance. The stone was quarried as huge blocks and transported to the site of construction place, which was a colossal task as we think of the technology during that period.

The temple is surrounded by an enclosing wall measuring 240 m (E-W) X 120 m (N-S). On plan the temple consists of the *garbhagriha*, *ardhamandapa*, *mahamandapa* and *mukhamandapa* and aligned on the east-west axis. The enclosure wall is adorned with a low two-storeyed cloistered structure on the inner side, marking the *prakara* of, the temple. This *prakara* is further enclosed by an outer *prakara* wall, which is further enclosed by a huge fortification wall of bricks. A moat encircles this fortification and the entire fortified area is known as Sivaganga Little Fort. On elevation, the temple consists of the *adhishthana*, *bhumi* (wall) portion divided into the upper and lower *bhumis*, followed by *prastara* (entablature) consisting of thirteen receding *talas*, *griva* (neck), *shikara* and surmounted by a *kalasha*.

Three gateways or *gopuras* could be observed here, namely the Rajarajan-tiruvasal (the innermost one), Keralantakan-tiruvasal (the middle gopura) and the outermost gateway. The Rajarajan-tiruvasal and the Keralantakam tiruvasal are completely built of granite and contemporary with the main temple. The Keralantakan-tiruvasal symbolises the victory of Rajaraja over the Cheras. The outermost *gopura* was constructed during the Maratha period in the eighteenth century. The Keralantakan-tiruvasal is slightly larger than the Rajarajan-tiruvasal. Both the gateways are richly carved and decorated with sculptural depictions of various gods and goddesses and divinities. The Rajarajan-tiruvasal depicts various Saivite episodes like the marriage of Siva and Parvati (Kalyanasundara), Siva protecting Markandeya (Markandeya-anugraha murti), Arjuna winning the pasupata weapon (Pasupata-anugraha murti). A large water body in the form of a tank, known as the Sivaganga tank is located to the north of the main temple and within the Sivaganga fort.

The *vimana* which rises to a height of 60.96 m rests on a high plinth measuring 45.72 metre square while the central shrine measures 30.48 metre square. The temple is the highest watermark in Dravidian temple order in terms of *vimana* construction. The *adhishthana* is fully adorned with inscriptions running all around. The *bhumi* portion which is nearly 13 metres in height, consists of niches on the south, west and north adorned, by deities like Siva, Vishnu and Durga. The lower niches on the southern side consist of Ganesa, Vishnu with Sridevi and Bhudevi, Lakshmi, Vishnuanugraha-murti, Bhikshatana, Virabhadra, Dakshina-murti, Kalantaka and Natesa.

The lower niches on the west consist of Harihara, Ardhanarisvara, two Chandrasekharas, one with and other without halo. On the northern side are Ardhanarisvara, Gangadhara, Virabhadra, Alingana-Chandrasekhara, Siva holding a spear, Sarasvati, Mahishamardini and Bhairava. The upper niches contain a series of Tripurantakas repeated several times. The depiction of Ganesa, Vrishavahana, Bhikshatana, Narasimha, Varaha is also found in the small circular space of the niche-tops.

After entering the temple complex through the inner *gopura* (Rajarajan-tiruvasal) there is a flight of steps leading to a pillared *mandapa.* The *mandapa* is a later addition and hence the temple originally did not have this provision. The two massive *dvarapalas* at the entrance once greeted the visitor. The *garbhagriha* is square on plan and consists of an interior and exterior wall and a passageway in between them forming a circumambulatory. The corbelled arch ceiling of the superstructure could be viewed from the upper ambulatory of the main sanctum.

The sanctum houses a huge linga. An inscription in the temple records it as Adavallan - one who dances well and Dakshinameru Vitankar, the name of the deity associated with Chidambaram. The deity at Chidambaram was greatly revered and worshipped by the Cholas and hence they named the deity at Brihadisvara with the same name. The deity is also known as Rajarajesvaram-udaiyar after the Chola Emperor and builder of this temple, Rajaraja.

The circumambulatory passage (the *pradakshinapata*) also houses three colossal sculptures of Siva. The walls of the *pradakshinapata* once contained narrative wall paintings of the period of Rajaraja I which was later covered by the later period (Nayak period) paintings of the 17th century AD. These two layers of paintings were noticed during a conservation measure at the temple and the Nayak period painting was carefully removed to expose the Chola period painting by the Archaeological Survey of India.

The Chola period paintings could be easily discernible from the Nayak period ones as the former are highly stylised and painted with subtle earth colours while the latter ones are cruder with black-outline and executed with bright colours. The theme of the Chola paintings is Saivitie, influenced by the lives of the Saiva saints, the Nayanmars. The Periyapuranam, a major literary work in Tamil, discusses in detail all the Nayanmars. Here, the life of Sundaramurti, one of the Nayanmars, is depicted as a mural on the west wall. In addition to this, on the western wall, Siva as Dakshina-murti is found depicted, shown seated on a tiger-skin in a yogic posture. Adjacent to the above image is a painting in which the devotees are shown depicted in front of a temple with Nataraja enshrined in it. On the other side of the wall is a painting in which a large figure of Nataraja is shown dancing in the golden hall at Chidambaram, while the devotees and priests on one side and a prince, identified as Rajaraja with his three queens along with followers are shown behind him. The painting of Rajaraja with his teacher Karuvur Devar is also depicted further up on the same wall.

The entire northern wall is depicted with a huge image of Tripurantaka Siva on a chariot driven by Brahma.

The upper ambulatory, directly above the lower ambulatory depicts various dance postures (karanas) of the Natya Sastra of Bharata performed by lord Siva. However only 81 of the 108 karanas are depicted here. The depiction of these karana postures is an important evidence for dance forms as early as Chola period indicating the codification of dance postures.

The temple is added with numerous subsidiary shrines after the construction of the temple. However, the Chandikesvara shrine located to the north of the *garbhagriha* and oriented on a north-south axis is contemporary to the main temple. The shrines like the great Nandi and the Nandi *mandapa* were added by the Nayaks in the 16th century AD; the Amman (goddess) shrine towards the northwest was added by the Pandyas in the 13th century AD; the Nataraja *mandapa* located towards the northeast and the Ganesha shrine located to the southwest were added by the Marathas in the 18th century AD. The Karuvur Devar or the Karuvurar shrine on the west and the richly decorated Subramanya shrine on the northwest were added by the Nayaks in the 17th century AD.

The construction of the Brihadeswara Temple at Thanjavur by Raja Raja I signifies a great transformation in the history of south India in the early years of the eleventh century with Thanjavur emerging as the stronghold of Tamil culture. The rise of the Chola empire and the consolidation of the political power by Raja Raja I resulted in creation of a sacred bhakti centre at Thanjavur with the Brihadeswara Temple dedicated to Shiva as Adavallan (Nataraja), tutelary deity of the Cholas, as its nucleus. This nucleus was clearly expressed by the magnitude of the temple complex and the soaring verticality of the vimana in particular. This was built on a monumental scale of which there is neither any precedence nor succession. Considering the outstanding universal value of this temple, this was inscribed as a World Heritage Site in the year 1987. This meticulously planned metaphorical and physical structure envisaged and implemented by Raja Raja I at Thanjavur was followed by subsequent rulers including his son Rajendra at Gangaikonda Cholapuram, as a continuing dynamic tradition. Subsequently in the same tradition, a temple was constructed at Darasuram. Each of this temple is a living temple having a well defined system of worship and rituals based on vedic traditions. In recognition of the fact that these three temples formed a unique group demonstrating a progressive development of high Chola architecture and art at its best, the UNESCO has inscribed all the three temples as World Heritage Sites under the caption "The Great Living Chola Temples" in the year 2004.

The Brihadeswara Temple at Thanjavur represents the zenith of the Dravida type of temples in its purest form, precision of conception and execution and magnitude of scale. Besides, it also represents the crystallisation of Tamil cultures; in its finest tradition of sculpture, painting, dance, music and literature.

References

Behera, K. S. (2005), *Konarak, the Black Pagoda*, Delhi.

Deva, Krishna (1990), *Temples of Khajuraho*, Archaeological Survey of India, New Delhi.

—— (1987), *Khajuraho*, ASI, New Delhi.

Donaldson, T. E. (1985), *Hindu Temple Art of Orissa*, II, Leiden.

Longhurst, A. J. (1924, 1928 and 1930), *Pallava Architectur*, Memoirs of the Archaeological Survey of India, Nos. 17, 33 and 40.

Mitra, D. (1992), *Konarak*, ASI, New Delhi.

Sivaramamurti, C. (1992), *The Chola Temples*, ASI, New Delhi.

Srinivasan, K. R. (1983), *Encyclopaedia of Indian Temple Architecture*, South India Lower Dravidadesa 200 BC-AD 1324, ASI, Delhi.

Srinivasan, K. R. (1972), *Temples of South India*, National Book Trust, New Delhi.

——(1985), *Temples of South India*, National Book Trust, Delhi.

Srinivasan, K. R. (1983), *Pallavas of Kanchi: Phase I*, Encyclopaedia of Indian Temple Architecture, South India Lower Dravidadesa 200 B.C.-A.D. 1324, Delhi.

Srinivasan, K. R. (1958), *The Pallava Architecture of South India*, Ancient India, No. 14, pp. 114-138, ASI, Delhi.

Srinivisan, K. R. (1964), *Cave Temples of the Pallavas*, ASI, New Delhi.

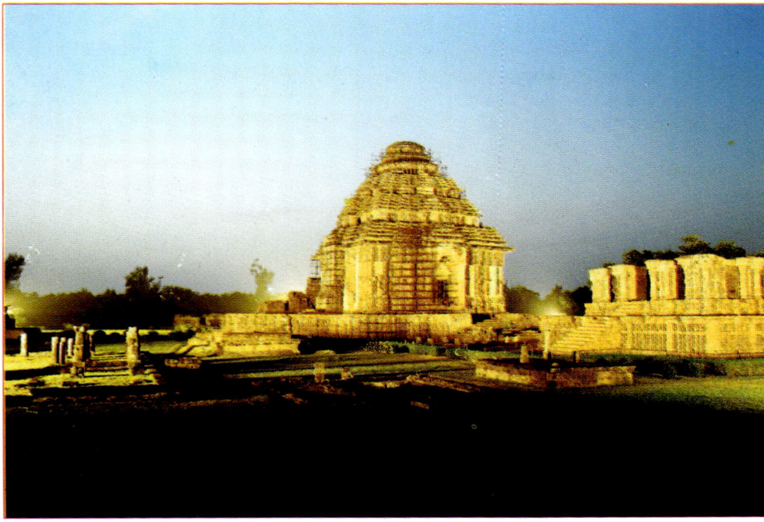

Sun Temple Konark

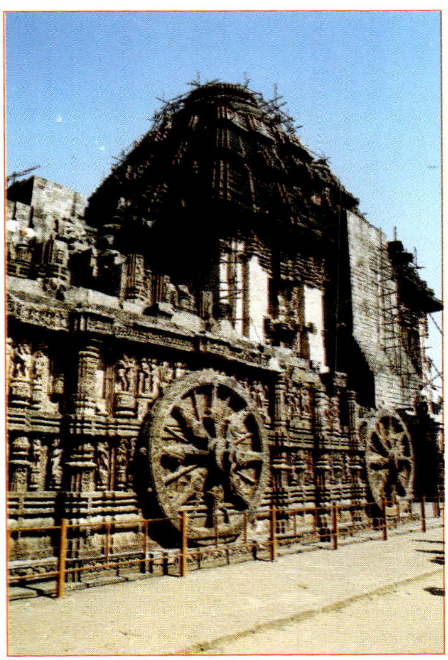

Sun Temple Konark

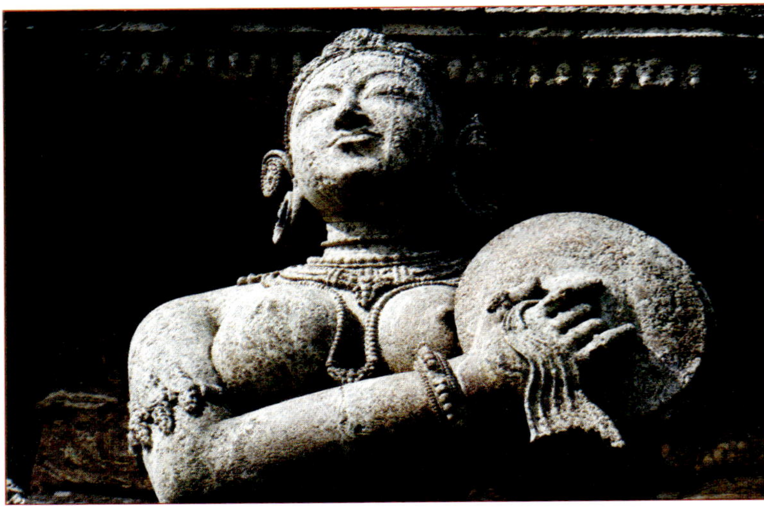

Lady Playing Cymbal Sun Temple Konark

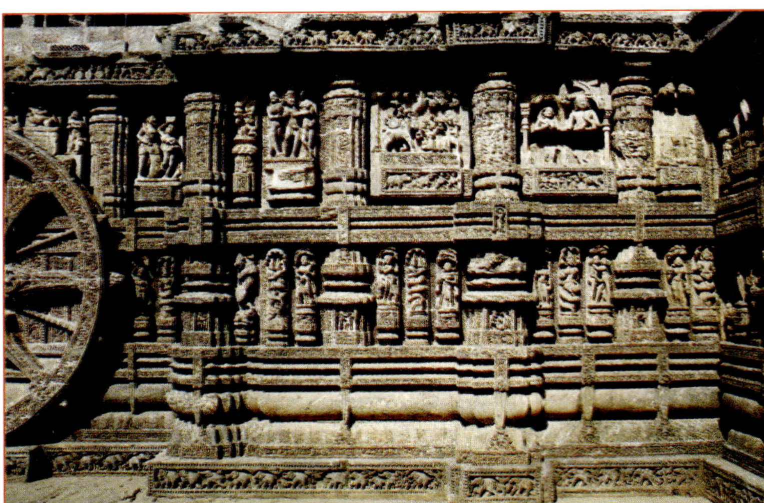

Sun Temple Konark

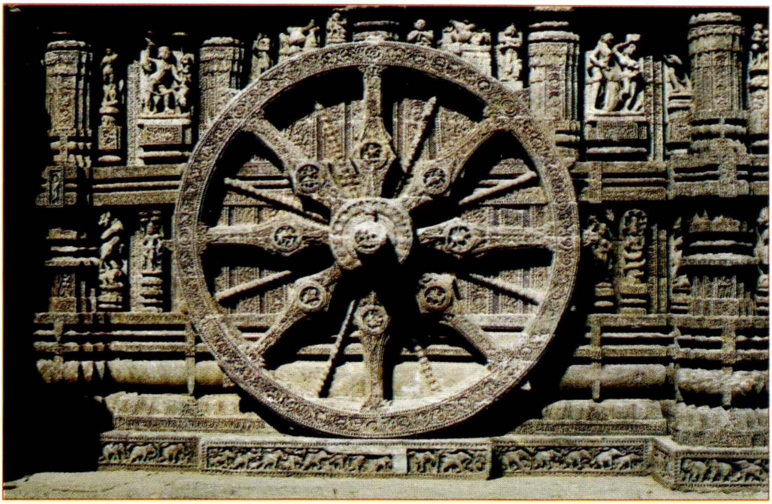

Konark Wheel

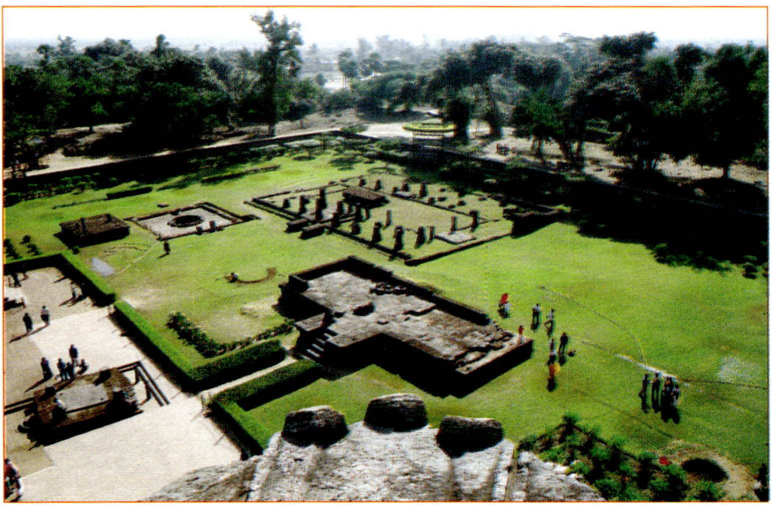

Minor Shrines in Konark Temple

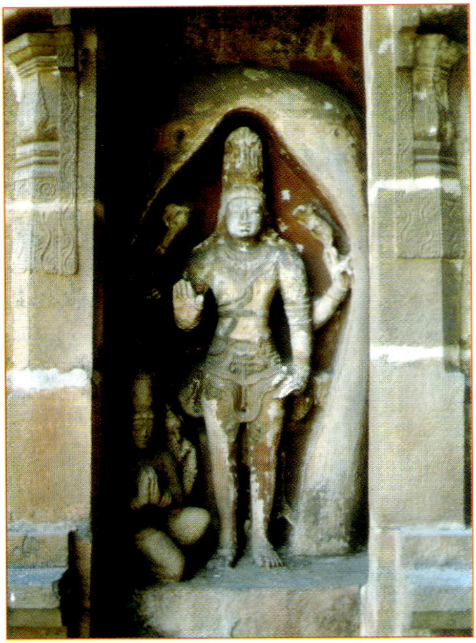

Siva (lingo abava) Brihadeswara temple complex Thajavur

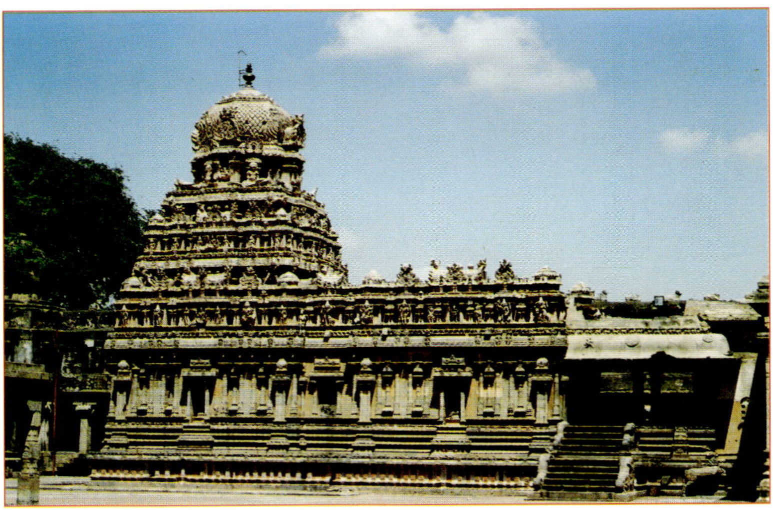

Subramanya temple Brihadewara Complex Thajavur

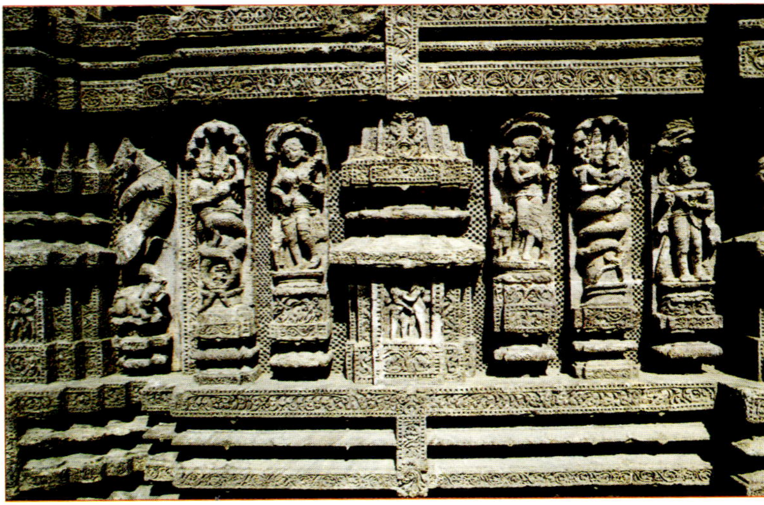

Sun Temple Konark

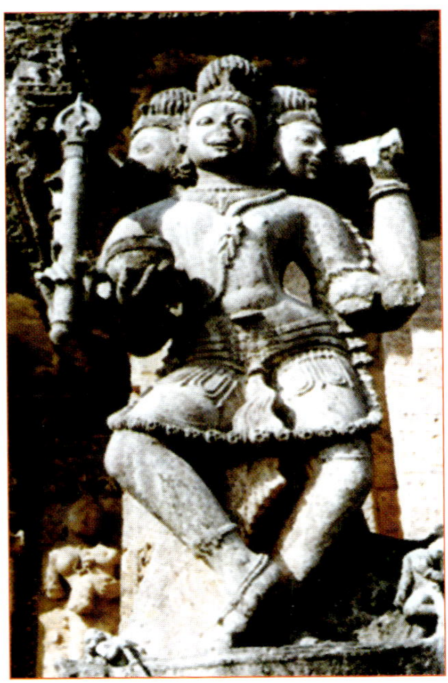

Bhairava Sun temple Konark

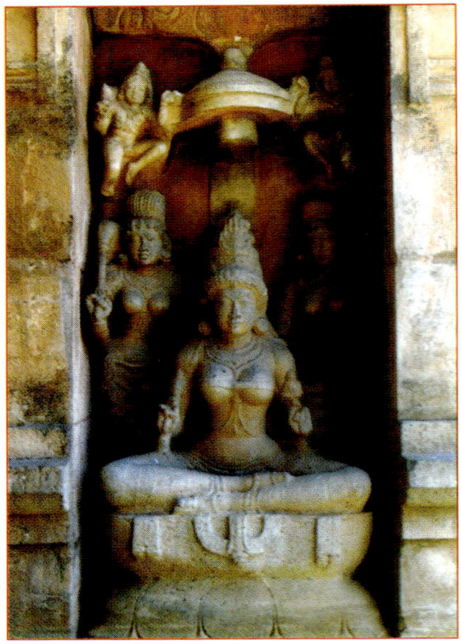

Brihadeawara temple Thanjavur

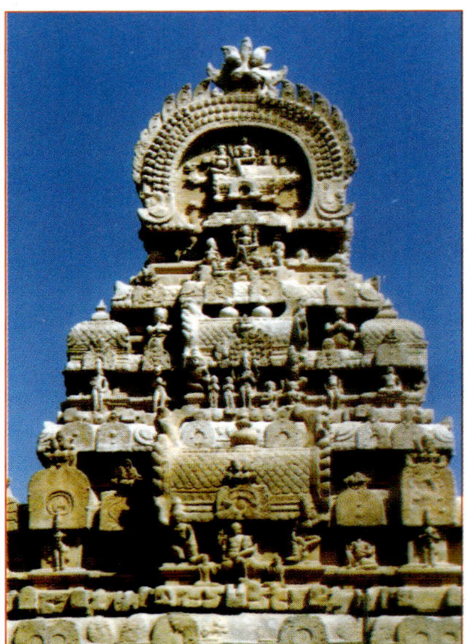

Brihadeawara temple Thanjavur

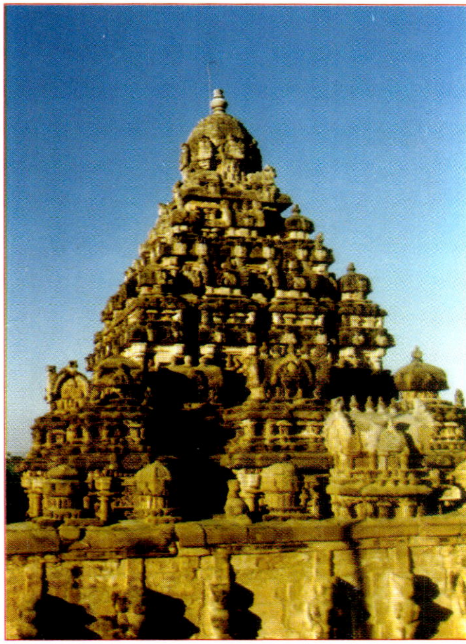

Kailashnath Temple (Kanchipuram)

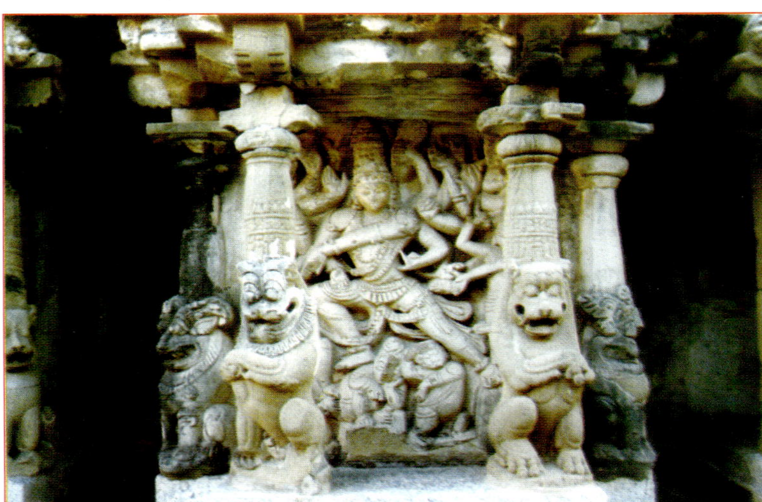

Kailashnath Temple (Kanchipuram)

2

Ajanta and Bagh Paintings

The Ajanta Caves are a major heritage site in the country. The very name "Ajanta" conjures up images of unparalleled beauty and artistic perfection; and a visit to the caves remains a milestone in the memory of any heritage lover. Among the ancient monuments of India, the rock cut caves of Ajanta have won this unique place because of the most perfect specimens of Indian mural paintings found in these caves. The renown of these caves is spread across the globe; and it is only second to the famous Taj Mahal in so far as the attraction of the international tourists and heritage lovers is concerned.

These caves are situated at a distance of 6.5 km from Fardapur, a village 101 km in the northern direction of Aurangabad in the State of Maharashtra. Fardapur is conveniently approached from Aurangabad and Jalgaon by motorable road. It is said that in 1819, a party of British soldiers of Madras Regiment on a hunting expedition chanced upon the Ajanta caves. The party was astounded not only by the caves, but also by the exquisite mural paintings found here, shrouded in the darkness of the caves. In cave 10 is the signature inscribed by John Smith on 28th April

1819 when he and his party of British soldiers chanced upon the caves while on a hunting expedition. The caves at Ajanta are excavated in the semi-circular scarp of a steep rock, about 76 m high, overlooking a narrow sinuous gorge through which flows the stream Waghora descending at the head of the ravine. The backdrop of the caves offers great scenic beauty. From the vantage place of the 'view point' when we look at the rocks, one can easily see that the caves have been excavated in the horse shoe shape. These caves which are Buddhist in origin were excavated for the use of monks during the rainy season (*Varsavasa*), when the monks had to take shelter in one place. One can very well imagine what sort of natural beauty would have descended on the place during the rains. However, on seeing Ajanta one can only reflect upon the famous words of the English poet, "A thing of beauty is a joy for ever." These are completely idyllic surroundings, cut off from the mundane world, providing not only a shelter to the monks, but also a completely spiritual world where the thoughts of the Buddha could only further flourish.

The caves, including the unfinished ones are thirty in number. The general arrangement of the caves was not pre-planned; and they have come up sporadically in various times. The floor-levels of the caves are not uniform, the lowest being Cave 8 and the highest being Cave 29. The caves of the earlier phase at Ajanta date from around the second century BC, and were excavated during the rule of Satavahana dynasty. Although the Satavahans were Hindu rulers, they also patronized Buddhist temples and monasteries. The early caves were also made by Hinyana Buddhists. Hinayana is the oldest sect of Buddhism, in which the Buddha was not represented in human form. He was worshipped through symbols such as the wheel, footprints and ri tual mounds like stupas. There are two types of caves, i.e. Chaityas and Viharas. The Chaityas are prayer halls and the Viharas are the monasteries for monks to live in. Out of the thirty caves mentioned, five (9, 10, 19, 26 and 29) are Chaitya-grihas and the rest are Viharas. The Cave Nos. 8, 9, 10, 12, 13 & 15 A belong to the earlier Hinyana phase of construction while the remaining ones belong to later (Mahayana) phase. Six centuries after the Hinyana caves were excavated, the Ajanta site witnessed a fresh burst of creative activity. These caves in the second phase were excavated in the fifth and sixth century AD under the benevolent rule of the Hindu Vakataka kings who were contemporaries of the Imperial Guptas. An inscription in Cave 16 states that Varahadeva, minister of king Harisena dedicates the caves to the Buddhist Sangha. By the time of the onset of the second creative phase in Ajanta, the Hinayana phase had given way to the Mahayana order. The Buddha was no longer represented only by symbols. Statues were now made depicting him in various distinctive 'mudras', like that of teaching or blessing, and a considerable Buddhist pantheon had evolved.

The caves at Ajanta present the finest specimens of rock-cut architecture in India. The earliest of the caves is the cave 10 which dates back to the second centrury BC. The following are the basic characteristics of the rock-cut caves. The *chaitya-grihas* are each characterized by a vaulted ceiling, the exterior facade being dominated by a huge horse-shoe shaped window, known as *chaitya* window, over the doorway. Internally they are divided by colonnades into central nave, an apse and side aisles, the latter continuing behind the apse, and thus, providing for circumambulation. At the center of the apse stands the object of worship in the form of a stupa hewn out of the live rock. During the second phase of excavation the general layout of the monasteries was standardized, although each one of them presents some interesting and individual features. The interior is treated with luxuriant carvings and the figure of Buddha appears on the Central Stupa - ani conism having by now given way to iconism. A profusion of figures of Buddha can be seen both on the facade and in the interior. The plan of the monasteries, however, shows greater innovations, the most important of which is the introduction of a shrine-chamber, containing a colossal image of Buddha in the back wall opposite the doorway, the monasteries thus serving the dual purpose of monastic dwelling and sanctuary.

However, the murals the paintings on the walls and the ceiling in the caves make the Ajanta caves so attractive and famous. In fact, the architectural quality and sculpture seldom receive attention in the presence of such luminous paintings. Whatever is left of these paintings surviving the ravages of time is in itself a great wonder, and a feast to the eyes. On the other hand, apart from the artistic value, the paintings also convey a great spiritual tradition, and has an ennobling impact on the sensitive human being who watches them with attention.

As already stated, the paintings also fall into two distinct creative phases. Some specimens of the earliest paintings survive in Caves 9 and 10, dating back to second century BC. The costumes of the figures, specially the headgear and ornaments resemble those in the bas-reliefs at Sanchi and Bharut. These paintings also indicate substantial artistic maturity. The second period of paintings which left its imprint in caves 1,2, 16 and 17 displays an exalted height and standard of art. The colour-scheme, expressiveness of the figures, the suppleness of the figures, and effective highlight bring out an impression of a very highly developed standard of painting during the period fourth-fifth century BC. The figures depicted are highly artistic and idealized, and the women figures have been shown in various beautiful poses and moods. They, in fact represent the best examples of mural paintings anywhere in the world.

The main theme of the paintings is the life of the Buddha, the Jataka stories. Therefore, the paintings veer around the Buddha, and the Bodhisattvas. They are intensly religious in tone. The entire drama of human life, from birth to death, all sufferings and pleasures have been portrayed. Also one finds the exposition of the entire society of those times from king to the beggar, prince to the pauper; men, women, children from all strata of human society in these paintings giving an impression of the totality of human society. The contemporary society of those times has been represented graphically, and in small details leaving nothing to imagination. There is also a full depiction of human emotions like passion, love, hatred, anger, compassion. Ultimately, however, the religious tone of the themes has to be appreciated as the underlying message behind the portrayal of human stories in the paintings.

The paintings on the walls are Jataka stories. But in the ceilings, the paintings are of a decorative nature. They are mostly flowers, plants, fruits, birds, beasts, human and semi-divine beings painted in a panorama to lend unmatched beauty to the ceilings of various caves.

Coming to the techniques of these paintings, it has to be stated that these are not done by fresco technique according to which pigments are mixed with water without any binding medium and applied on a fresh wet lime-plaster. In case of the Ajanta paintings, the ground was first prepared by laying a rough layer of ferruginous earth, mixed with rock grit or sand, vegetable fibres, paddy-husk, grass and other fibrous material of organic origin, on the surfaces of walls and ceilings. A second coat of mud and ferrugenious earth was then applied. Finally the surface was finished with a coat of limewash. On this surface the outlines of the paintings were drawn boldly, and then spaces were filled with requiste colours in different shades and tones. The colour scale was simple and limited consisting of red and yellow ochre, lime, kaolin, gypsum, lapis lazali (blue) and lamp black. These basic colours were locally available except lapis lazuli which was imported from Badaksham region of modern Afghanistan. The binding medium has been generally identified as glue.

The painters of these caves belonged to professional guilds. They were extremely devout, although not necessarily belonging to the Buddhist faith. A painter was almost a yogi totally lost in his art. "He created his masterpieces not in the spirit of imposing his personality on an admiring world with a desire for personal honour or fame, but obliterated himself, almost deriving supreme satisfaction in that his art was an offering to God," so writes Dr. C. Sivaramamurti in his translation of the chitrasutra of the Vishnudharmottara. It is this sublime sense of humility and devotion which is the principal spirit of the artist in the paintings. When one stands before the paintings and starts appreciating them, one can try to visualize the intense concentration and devotion with which the painter must have painted these masterpieces which have stood the test of time. Also it should be appreciated how truly and genuinely the emotions of human beings have been brought out. The feeling of caring, love, and other emotions come flowing freely from these figures. The painter must have created the works in a state of 'ecstasy'. If one stands for long in real concentration before the paintings, 'ecstasy is what develops in the mind and the heart. The concern of the painter here not merely depicted the physical world. It goes beyond. The figures depicted in the murals always look within. They are searching within for a life and they are in that sense intensely withdrawn. The physical features like face, arms and other parts of the body are suffused with that inner beauty also. As one looks for long at the famous painting of Padampani in Cave one can watch and slowly absorb the serenity in the face of "the Bodhisattva holding the lotus" which is only reflection of the inner divinity within the figure. In Ajanta, the painters have been able to bring out the beauty of the external form no doubt; but more importantly, the inner feelings of contentment, search and divine connectivity have been successfully depicted. It only means that the creator of the art had put his heart and soul in the work of art, thus becoming one with his creation. The impact of the individual figures in an artistic sense is quite compelling; on the other hand, the totality of impression in a spiritual sense, is even more profound.

The highly narrative style of the paintings is another aspect to be noted. The paintings are mostly of the Jataka Stories, of the various lives of the Buddha. Therefore, the sequence of events in various births has been reflected in a highly narrative way. Moreover, the individual Jatakas have not been formally demarcated, indicating a continuity of the stories. Time has been represented in the paintings in a highly unified and continuous way, breaking the barriers of the past, present and future. The paintings also show a high degree of technical sophistication. Although no shadows are there in the paintings, the various nuances have been successfully highlighted. By the conscious deepening and lighting of the colours, the brilliant effect of highlighting expressive body parts like eyelids, nose, lips and chin has been achieved. One can easily notice that the beauty of the human form, and in fact all other forms of life and nature have been so nicely brought out. There is nothing jarring, not missing note in these paintings. It is a highly idealized world, full of beauty and wonder; and finally it conveys an ultimate expression of joy, as if to reiterate the message that "a thing of beauty is a joy for ever".

The murals of the Ajanta are the richest remaining jewels of the ancient art of India. Similar paintings are also there in caves at Kanheri, Bhaja, Bagh, Ellora and Badami. However, the paintings in Ajanta have to this day remained as the leading light of these mural paintings indicating the richest phase of our ancient history of art. The Archaeological Survey of India which took over the care of the caves after independence has made many efforts to preserve and conserve the paintings. Earlier the Nizam of Hyderabad had this charge who could not take effective steps for preservation. Besides, the Ajanta caves have been inscribed by UNESCO as World Heritage Sites, and international attention has been bestowed upon the conservation of these caves and the mural paintings. They are a pride of our ancient heritage. But very vigorous efforts are required to preserve them.

Murals in the Principal Caves and the Jataka Stories

Cave 1: At the beginning of the horseshoe bend on the northside of the Ajanta site is the most magnificient *vihara* In India. This cave is a place of sheer beauty and grace in which the painter has attained the highest standards of artistic excellence. Every painting here conveys the painter's devotion to his task. The portico of the cave has collapsed long back. As of now, there is a verandah, a large hall and a shrine in the back. There are 20 pillars. In the sanctum there is a colossal image of the Buddha seated in *dharma-chakra-pravartana - mudra* (preaching attitude). The cave contains some of the masterpieces of paintings in the world. The figures of the Bodhisattvas full bodied and majestic, yet pouring karuna (compassion) painted on the back wall of the inner aisle, are of special attraction. The Bodhisattva on the left holds a lily. He is the famous 'Padmapani', a figure of immense, ethereal beauty. Watching the eyelids lowered and in divine introspection is an experience that is unbelievable. This a highly gentle figure, standing serene and introspective in the midst of myriad worldly activities. Next to the Bodhisattva Padmapani is painted a dark princess holding a lotus - an indication that she is his consort. Her face has a calm expression and she possesses exquisite limbs. It is indeed a highly graceful painting.

On the right of the entrance to the anti-chamber of the main shrine of cave 1 is the majestic figure of the Bodhisattva Vajrapani, who bears the thunderbolt. The glorious workmanship of the jewelled crown of the Bodhisattva Vajrapani is indeed remarkable. The painting of the Bodhisattva Vajarapani is a masterpiece of the Ajanta art, and reveals the majesty of spirit in full glory.

Inside the main hall on the right hand side one of the capitals is subtly carved to create the illusion of four recumbent and standing deer sharing a single head. This has been so cleverly done that it looks consistent and realistic.

The two sidewalls of the antechamber depict two important incidents from the Master's life. The one on the left represents the Assault and Temptation of Mara on the eve of the Buddha's enlightenment. When Gautama took his seat in Vajrasana, with determination not to get up until achieving enlightenment, Mara, the evil one employed all means to thwart his determination and attacked him with his army. But Gautama remained unmoved and invoked the Earth to bear witness to his right to the Vajrasana. This silenced Mara who fled discomfited. Here Gautama is seen in his bhumisparsamudra, touching the earth. Then Mara used his beautiful daughters to seduce Gautama, and this effort also failed. The right wall of the antechamber is painted with the miracle of Sravasti. In order to confound the six heretical teachers, Buddha performed a few miracles in the presence of a group of spectators headed by king Prasenjit of Sravasti. One of the miracles was his multiplying himself into innumerable Buddhas in different mudras, poised on lotuses.

The walls of the hall are painted with J ataka stories, prominent among which are "Sibi Jataka," the story of king Sibi who went to the extent of giving his own flesh to uphold justice, 'Sankhapala Jataka', the story of the Bodhisattva born as naga (serpent) king, and 'Mahajanaka Jataka' depicting the story of the king of Mithila taking the path of renuciation. Also depicted in the Cave 1 is the story of conversion of Nanda, a cousin of Gautama who left palace life and turned a mendicant.

The Jataka stories depict the various births of the Buddha. It may be noted that many of the births are those of animals; not every birth was human. In the paintings of Ajanta there is a total unity of human life and animal life. The unity of all forms of life has been vividly depicted.

On the wall of the cave 1 is also depicted the Champeya Jataka, the story of Bodhisattva Naga king Champeya giving sermons to king Ugrasena, about the righteous path.

Cave 2 is also like Cave 1 a beautifully painted Vihara. It is smaller; and the main hall contains 12 pillars which are richly carved. The back wall of the shrine is carved with the figure of Buddha in darma-chakra-pravartana mudra. There are many inscriptions. One of the beautiful verses inscribed is as follows:

> Blossoms are the ornaments of trees, it is flashes of lightning that adorn the big rain clouds, the lakes are adorned by lotuses and waterlilies with their intoxicated bees; but virtues brought to perfection are the proper ornaments of living beings.

This cave is highly decorated. All the walls and the ceiling are exquisitely painted. The paintings on the ceilings take the form of compartments filled in with a variety of designs, floral patterns, birds, fruits, flying figures, fantastic and comic figures, and geometric and ornamental motifs. The painting on the ceiling of the shrine is one of the best specimens of painter's art in Ajanta. The painter has shown his masterly execution in the delineation of a procession of twenty-three geese in various attitudes which *forms* part of the ceiling-painting of the chapel to the left of the antechamber. On the rear wall are rows of seated Buddha figures in different postures. These figures are seated on lotuses. They are lively and expressive, and not repetitive depictions. From the life of Buddha, the dream of Maya who dreamt about a white elephant entering her body, the interpretation of her dream, and Bodhisattva in the Tushita heaven before his descent have been painted in cave 2. Hansa Jataka, and Vidurapandita Jataka have also been painted.

Cave 9 is a *Chaitya-griha* dating back to the first century BC. It belongs to the earlier phase of the caves, containing a nave, an apse and aisles by a collonade of twenty-three pillars. At the centre of the apse stands a globular stupa on a high cylindrical base. There are two layers of paintings at two places. A later painting is superimposed on an earlier painting without completely rubbing off the earlier painting. The figures of the Buddha appear as later paintings although in the earlier phase the *Chaitya-griha* was dedicated to the Hinyana faith.

Cave 10 also belongs to the category of earliest *Chaitya-grihas*, and is much larger than cave 9. Inscriptions reveal that the *Chaitya* dates back to second century BC. Like Cave 9, this cave also contains two layers of paintings. Two J ataka stories have been painted. The Sama Jataka' is the story of Bodhisattva born as "Sama", the sole support of his blind parents who was shot by the king of Varanasi. The 'Chhaddanta Jataka' is the story of Bodhisattva born as Chhaddanta, a six tusked royal elephant who was magnanimous enough to allow his tusks to be sawed off for the queen of Varanasi. In Cave 10 is inscribed the signature of John Smith on 28th April 1819, when he and his party of British soldiers chanced upon the caves while out on a hunting expedition. On the walls and pillars of this cave there are many donative inscriptions by monks who would have provided for the paintings.

Next we can mention Cave 16 which is one of the most beautiful monasteries, (*Viharas*). Inscription on the left side wall outside the verandah rec'ords the dedication of this magnificient dwelling excavated in the caves for the use of 'best of ascetics' by Varahadeva, the minister of the Vakataka king Harsena. This cave has twenty pillars. Inside the shrine is the gigantic image of Budha in teaching attitude (*Dharma Chakra Pravartana mudra*), seated in *Pralamba Padasana* posture. This image is carved in high relief and has a circumambulatory passage around it. Most of the paintings in this cave have disappeared. Of the surviving paintings, one is identified as the story of conversion of Nanda, and the other is Sujata's offering of Pay as a, Buddha with his begging bowl on a city street, and the dream of Maya. The Hasti Jataka and Maha-ummagga Jataka have been painted also. But most of the paintings have been damaged.

Cave 17 is again a magnificient Vihara. In the splendid cave the walls are adorned with a profusion of painted stories. In the antechamber the image of the Buddha is seated in *dharma-chakra-pravartana mudra*, detached from the back wall of the shrines. Budha is also flanked by the figures of Padmapani and Vajrapani. This monastery which has preserved the greatest number of murals, is noted for a number of masterpieces. Almost the entire surface of the walls and the ceiling of this cave has been painted. The paintings on the ceiling feature skillfully executed modulations to give the impression of the cloth canopy of a shamiana. A number of Jataka stories have been reflected in the paintings on the walls of this cave. There is the painting of Vessentara J ataka, the story of Vessentara, the generous prince who was the last birth of Bodhisattava before his enlightenment as the Buddha. The other Jatakas painted are Chhaddanta Jataka, Mahakapi Jataka, Hasti Jataka and Hansa Jataka. In all these Jataka paintings, the various births of Bodhisattva have been told in which he displayed selfless sacrifice for the good of others. In cave 17, seventeen Jataka stories have been depicted through paintings. Also of particular beauty are the paintings of apsaras in the panel to the right of the door which reveal the consummate skill of the artist. The back wall of the antechamber to the left of the door, depicts Buddha's wife Yashodhara putting forward Rahula, the latter begging his patrimony of Buddha who puts forward his begging bowl.

Cave 17 therefore turns out to be one of the magnificiently painted caves, containing the paintings of a very lage number of Jataka stories told from the various births of Bodhisattva. The portrayal of the Apsara is highly sophisticated and exquisite.

Cave 19 is a well-proportioned Chaitya griha, and it belongs to the later period of excavation dated to fifth century AD. This is a Chaitya griha of Mahayana faith. The plan of the older Chaitya grihas has been retained with the singular difference that now the human image of Buddha is found in the place of the earlier votive stupa of Hinayana faith. The walls of the hall are painted with figure of Buddha in different panels; the one on the left wall representing Buddha giving his begging-bowl to Rahula, the latter put forward by his mother Yashodhara.

Cave 26 contains two important portrayals. One is the *mahaparinirvana* of Buddha, carved on the left wall near the side door, which contains a colossal figure of Buddha reclining on his right side on a couch between two sala trees; below are the figures of his disciples and followers mourning his decease, and above are celestial beings. The second scene is the temptation of Mara in which Buddha is seated in *Bhumisparsamudra*, and on the left Mara's attack has been shown along with allurements of Mara' s daughters on the right.

In many of the caves, the paintings have disappeared due to vagaries of nature. Some of the caves have remained incomplete. Whatever survives is unique and spectacular, and reveals the noble artistic traditions of those times. The paintings of Ajanta are finest specimens of art, and the themes of Buddhism painted lends a noble spiritual content. The paintings are extremely beautiful; but not merely in a mundane way; there is a divinity in these paintings which strikes the discerning observer. The paintings have been made in a mood of devotion, and an attitude of worship. Ajanta paintings, therefore, remain the most important destination of cultural tourism in the country. A journey to Ajanta and nearby Ellora caves is not merely a travel in search of magnificient art, but a spiritual journey of unforgettable dimensions.

The Archaeological Survey of India has a big challenge of ensuring that the paintings which have survived the ravages of time are preserved. There are current and real dangers to the structural stability of many caves. The rain water is coming down on the slope of the top of caves causing continuous damage. Rain water is also entering the caves through various cracks and fissures in the rock. The Japan International Corporation Agency (JICA) is assisting a project for preservation of these and other Buddhist caves near by. The UNESCO has appointed a panel of Experts (POE) under the JICA Project to take urgent technical decisions. Italian experts are being consulted for preservation of paintings. But ultimately, ASI has to be exceptionally alert to preserve and protect the caves, and also the invaluable paintings which are a glowing testimony of the ancient art of India.

Cave Paintings of Bagh

The Buddhist caves of Bagh are situated in Dhar Distt. of Madhya Pradesh, on the bank of the Baghini river, a tributary of the river Narmada. There are nine rock-cut caves excavated on sandstone cliff of Vindhya hills. The main caves have quadrangular plan and consist of a vihara or central hall with a stupa filled sanctum in the near, forming a small Chaitya griha or chapel. The sides have small cells for the monks while the façade is a colonnaded portico. Generally speaking, the Bagh caves have a great affiliation with contemporary caves at Ajanta and Pitalkhora, but there are differences. The Chaitya griha is conspicuous by its absence. It seems that the monastery chapel served the purpose of the chaitya hall. Secondly, the stupas in caves 2 and 4 at Bagh are plain and do not have sculpted images of the Buddha on them unlike the stupas in the chaitya grihas of Deccan caves.

As at Ajanta, in the Bagh caves also, the walls and the ceilings were profusely ornamented with beautiful paintings. The paintings of Bagh are executed in tempera. Analysing the technique of the paintings Marshall writes.

At Bagh, as at Ajanta, the paintings are done in tempera, not, as has often been stated, in fresco, and the process and colours employed at both places seem to have been the same. At Bagh, however, less care has been taken over the preparation of the first, rough coat. As at Ajanta this coat is made of the local ferruginous earth compounded with gravel, lime and the fibres of jute and hemp. The work, however, has been done in a somewhat slipshod manner, and as a consequence, the rinfazzo is less tenacious than at Ajanta-a defect that has contributed in no small measure to the deterioration of the paintings.

The colours used at Bagh are earth colours like red-ochre, yellow ochre and terraverte; mineral colours like lapis lazuli for blue and lime for white. Black derived from carbon is the only chemical colour. While the red pigment is of a somewhat fugitive nature and has flaked off at places, the blue is of a more enduring nature and is ubiquitous at Bagh.

Most of the caves have been exacavated in porous sandstone, and owing to the poor quality of the rock many of the pillars, walls and roofs have collapsed. Some of the caves have become inaccessible being chocked by their own debris. A Committee of Experts led by the ASI had studied the problem of conservation of the caves, and as a result of the Committee's recommendation, some headway was made in structural conservation and chemical preservation. The entire upper rock surface was profusely grouted by drilling holes which were filled with cement. Many of the damaged sculptures of the Buddha and Bodhisattva were repaired. In order to make the caves accessible a bridge has been constructed over the river. From the study of the inscription on a land grant copper plate discovered in the debris of the Cave 2, and also after studying the inconographic features of the sculptures, it is surmised that the date of the caves can be put to mid 5th century AD. The Bodhisattva paintings combining both sensuous and spiritual features indicated the developed art of the mature Gupta period. There are, of course, theories to suggest that the caves dated back to 2nd and 3rd Century AD.

Cave 4 was the most magnificient cave in Bagh, and the whole cave was covered with plaster and originally profusely decorated with paintings. The front of the cave was protected by a continuous varandah; but the roof of the verandah later collapsed exposing the paintings to inclement weather. Fortunately, faithful copies of original paintings were made by master artists like Nand Lal Bose, Haldar, etc. in the early decades of the 20th Century. The interpretation of the main scenes of painting which have survived has long puzzled art historians. Vogel frankly admits that he is not able to reconstruct anything except that it is possibly some Jataka or Avadana. John Anderson identifies it as the Mahajanaka Jataka shown at Ajanta. However, the sequence of scences depicted of this Jataka at Ajanta is very different from those at Bagh. The only thing that is common is the dance scene, but even there also there exist di fferences, The other scenes depicted are as follows:

1. Two women seated in an open pavillion one of whom is weeping and the other consoling her.
2. Four men seated in a grove hearing sermons from an ascetic.
3. A group of flying monks.
4. Two groups of beautiful women singing and dancing with a male figure in the centre.
5. Another scene of preaching involving two male figures.

This panel of paintings is identified as the story of Nanda and Sundari. Nanda was the half brother of Buddha, and he was full of passion for his beautiful wife Sundari. He was converted to Buddhism, but not before he had to go through several events, since he could not curb his passion. He was taken by the Buddha to Indra's paradise where he was smitten with passion for the Apsaras, and he forgets his love for Sundari. Finally, however, he understands the futility of his desires and passion, and gets converted to Buddhism. Asvaghosa has brilliantly described this story in his *Saundarananda*. The Bagh paintings have followed closely the story line of *Saundarananda* in which Asvaghosa, has given a full description of the history of Kapilavastu, and how Gautama and Nanda being half-brothers showed contrary tendencies from their childhood. Nanda was given to the pleasures of the world, whereas Gautama was sensitive to the sorrow and sufferings of life. The paintings of two women, one weeping, another consoling, the sermon in the grove, the flying monks, the singing and dancing celestial women, and the last preaching scene (Ananda giving sermon to Nanda) are interpreted as various espisodes of Saundrananda of Asvaghosa.

Aesthetic and Spiritual Dimensions

In appreciating the aesthetic dimensions of the paintings in Bagh, and of course Ajanta and other contemporary caves, one sees how artistic expression in ancient India was integrally combined with religious values. This was also so with other art forms and performing arts. This was, therefore, not secular art, but art with the purpose of expressing, and manifesting strong religious and spiritual values of those times. A question may be asked whether the autonomy of the art form, and its creative fulfillment are affected by the expression of religious thoughts for which the artistic creations become vehicles. It was however, not considered proper that art should become merely an ornamental or decorative form. It was of the essence of art that it should suggest something beyond itself.

In the ancient Indian tradition, art was not for art sake; it was for Dharma. The works of art were always part of some belief systems, faith and religion, and finally, the objective of art was spiritual. It is against this philosophy that the paintings of Ajanta and Bagh have to be appreciated. If we examine Buddhistic art forms, we find that the teachings of the Buddha were against song, dance and other forms of enjoyment, as these were opposed to the discipline of monastic order. The Buddha was indifferent to the body. During the period of Ashoka, who spread the teachings of Buddhism, the visual art forms consisted mainly of the famous Asokan pillars. The Buddha images emerged only between 1 st century BC and 1 st century AD in Gandhara and Mathura. It is only thereafter that the initial fear of sensuous form as a distraction from Buddhist meditation was overcome, and Buddhist iconography developed, reaching its perfect form in the Gupta period between 4th century and 6th century AD. A synthesis of the sensuous and the spiritual was accomplished; and in the Ajanta and Bagh paintings this was clearly manifested. To any form of art, there is a dimension of 'rupa' which is the objective aspect, and there is 'rasa' which comes out of the subjective appreciation of art. The full appreciation of art moves between the two polarities of 'rupa' and 'rasa', between the objective and the subjective; and between the visible and the invisible. The first effect of art is to attract and focus the mind on the 'rupa' thus removing the distraction of the mind. Once the distraction is removed, the next effect is to bring for the mind a level of absorption which results in a generalized consciousness, which is neither in the subject, nor in the object; neither in the observer, nor in the observed, which one can describe as 'rasa'. This sublime combination of 'rupa' and 'rasa' has been fully achieved in these paintings.

These have therefore become masterpieces of art, radiating beauty and creativity, which are firmly rooted in the earth, and yet transcendental in consciousness.

References

Behl, Binoy K., *The Ajanta Caves: Ancient Paintings of Buddhist India*, Thames and Hudson.

Mitra, Debala (1980), *Ajanta*, ASI, New Delhi.

Pande, Anupa (2002), *The Buddhist Cave Paintings of Bagh*, New Delhi, Aryan Books International.

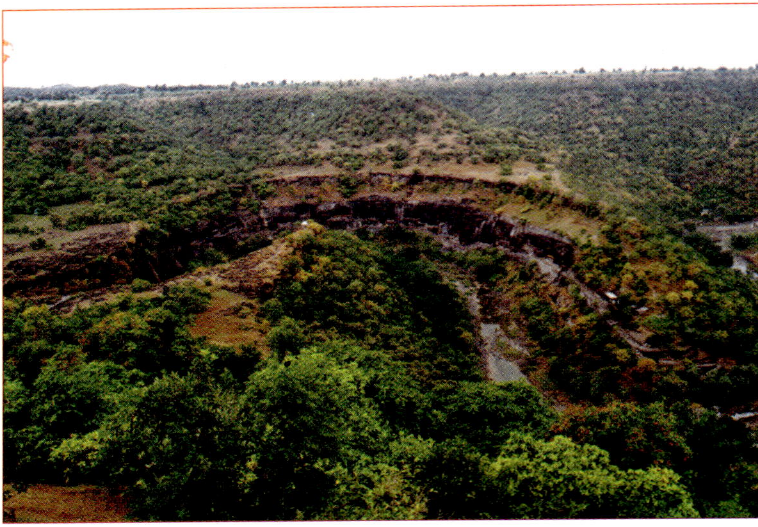

Ajanta Cave from view Point

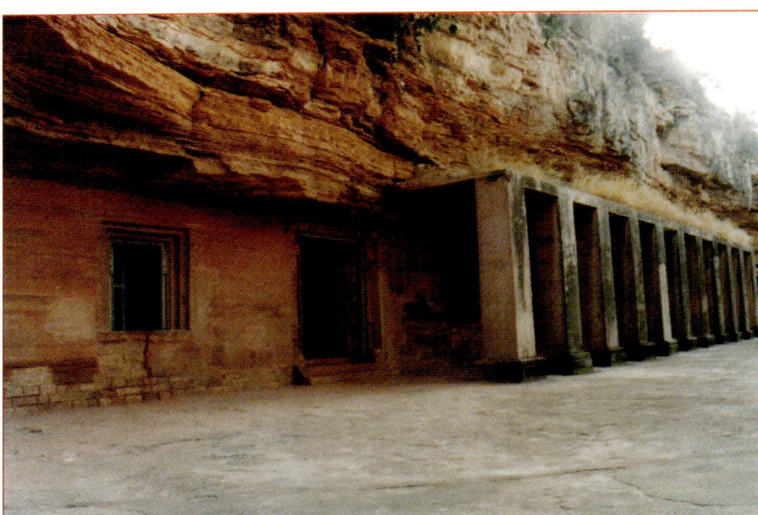

Bagh Caves

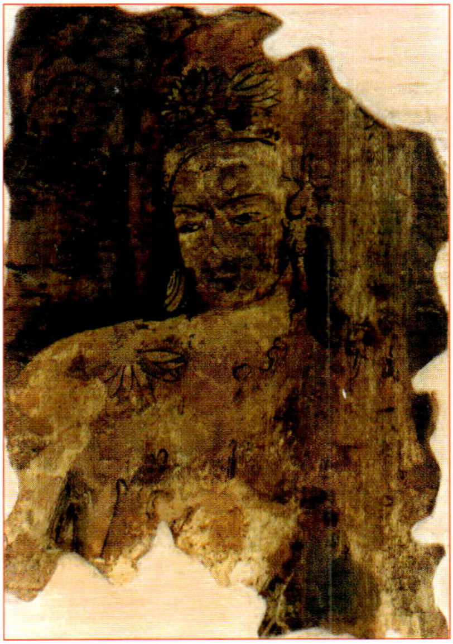

Bodhisattva Bagh Caves

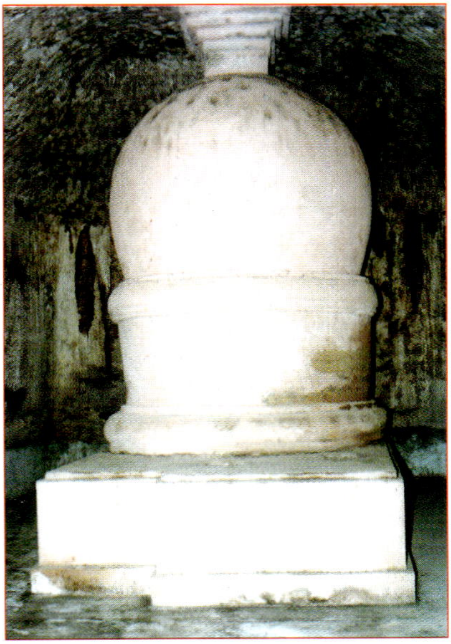

Stupa Bagh Caves

3

Sculptures of Kushana Period

The Kushanas, one of the most prominent Indian dynasties were of foreign, central Asian origin. They are also known as Scythians, Sakas, Yuch-Chih, and were part of a protracted nomadic migration that began on the western borders of China. The Yuch-Chih, who dwelt in the area between Tuan-huang and Chi-lien (Western Kansu) sometime before the second-century BC, were attacked by the Hsiung-nu. This provoked their migration in a westerly direction. Subsequently they divided into two groups. The main group moved towards the northern borders of the Gobi desert; and the lesser horde went south and settled in the Tibetan borderlands and the khotan area. The main group of nomads invaded the homeland of the Sakas, situated, north of the Oxus river. The Kushanas then invaded Bactria. The conquest of Bactria is supposed to have happened completely by the year 122 BC. The Kushana empire came into prominence shortly before the Christian era under the rule of Kujula Kadphises. From the inscriptions it is gathered that the 'Saka era' or 'Saka Samvat' which starts in AD 78 was founded by Kanishka, the most prominent ruler of the Kusana dynasty. Kanishka established his rule over the north-western territories as well as Punjab and the Gangetic basin with Peshawar and Mathura as the capital cities. His reign marked a developed period of Indian civilization. Not only was he a protector of art and scholarship, associated with figures such as Asvaghosa, but he was also a tolerant promoter of religions. Buddhism was the most prominent religion which eventually spread to Central Asia and the Far East, thus spreading Indian culture far beyond the border of the Kushana empire.

The Kushana king Kanishka was not only a powerful ruler but also a patron of art and scholarship. His empire encompassed some of the area of the great trade routes between the Mediterranean and India and China, and because of easy access to ports in the Indus Delta, navigation and diplomatic relations between India and Rome were possible. This helped in the development of an eclectic intellectual, religious and cultural life in the early centuries in India. The Kushanas were invaders - a migratory people of great strength, but little culture. But because of this situation as described above, highly developed artistic trends came into evolution. They were expressed in two main forms of sculpture; Mathura and Gandhara.

The Mathura style which flourished around the town of Mathura, one of the leading centres of art and culture those days developed from the indigenous Indian traditions which started from the Maurya and Sunga/Satavahana art forms covering the period of history between third to 1st century BC. The Gandhara school, on the other hand, flourished in the north-western region of India, now Pakistan and Afghanistan, with Peshawar and Taxila as its main centres. The Gandhara art form was in eclectic style in which the Greco-Roman style predominated. It was therefore a great period of art and sculpture, when on both eastern and western parts of the Kushana empire, two distinctive styles flourished and thus represented a high point in the cultural history of India.

The Kushanas were nomadic invaders who originally did not have anything to do with culture. But they established a rule over ancient India which lasted for about three hundred years, and witnessed a tremendously powerful art movement which not only thrived on the indigenous traditions, but also borrowed from the external influences, thus constituting a unique period in India's art history.

The Kushana empire was well known for prosperity in trade and commerce. Since the empire connected the trade routes between the Mediterranean and China, the Kushanas maintained close ties with Rome. This is evidenced by the adoption of Roman gold standard by the Kushanas, and also regular sending of Kushana emissaries to Roman court, beginning with Augustus' reign (27 BC-14 AD), and beyond. As trade and commerce brought in prosperity, the Kushana empire also became a cradle for the promotion of art, culture, intellectual and spiritual development. The Kusanas did not have a cultural tradition of their own but they had great adaptability. They adapted themselves to the prevailing cultural traditions. Thus they promoted two distinct schools of art, Mathura, and Gandhara, the former indigenously rooted, and the later mostly derived from Greco-Roman traditions.

Mathura was in those days a prosperous city situated in the Ganga Yamuna basin. It was on the ancient trade route between Pataliputra and Taxila. The city had a cosmopolitan character, since the traders while passing through the city stayed for considerable periods of time contributing to the cosmopolitanism, and religious as well as racial tolerance.

The Buddhist text of Lalitavistara describes how large and prosperous was the city of Mathura. The city is also mentioned in Mahabharata and Puranic literature, being associated with the birth of Krishna, the divine incarnation of God according to the Hindu traditions. Ptolemy had described Mathura as a "City of Gods" It was a major centre of religion in those times; and Buddhism, Jainism and Brahmanism flourished there side by side. Mathura continued for long as a major centre of cultural diversity, and religious pluralism. There was a long tradition of worship of semi-divine nature spirits, such as yaksas, nagas and *salabhanjikas*. Along with other motifs and religious symbols, these divine spirits also became the subject of scriptural representation. Mathura continued as an active centre for arts and culture contemporaneously with Sanchi and Bharut. But most vital and creative period of this art was under the Kushana rule between the first and third century AD. There was active patronage of the Kushanas; and also the spread of Buddhism lent the art of Mathura its special distinction. Around the mid-third century the Sassanian invasion reduced the power of the Kusanas. But the Mathura school, after this lull revived again during the rule of the Gupta dynasty from the second quarter of the fourth century AD. through the following three centuries. However, Hinduism had become a stronger force by that time, and the Hindu Bhakti traditions now dominated the Mathura school of art.

The several types of Buddhist structures that existed in Mathura include the *stupa*, *vihara*, *sangharama* (monasteries), and the *chaitya*. The most important archaeological finds were provided by the mounds of Jamalpur, Bhateswar, Katra, Chaubara, Palikhera, Maholi, Ganesra, Govindnagar, and others.

Two important Jaina stupas were located on the site of Kankali Tila and and in addition, there is evidence of early Brahmanical shrines.

Alexander Cunnigham began excavating these mounds after the initial discovery by Stacy in 1836 of the first Mathura sculpture known as Silenus, presently, in Indian Museum in Calcutta. A number of excavations carried out on a regular basis from the 1850s by General Cunningham, Bhagvanlal Indraji, F.S. Growse, Alois Anton Fuhrer, Radha Krishna and others revealed an astonishing variety and wealth of sculptural material. The excavations which have continued till date are constantly revealing new material to enrich the knowledge of that period. Excavations were conducted in Sonkh by Dr. Herbert Hartel, and in Govindnagar by Dr. R.C. Sharma under the auspices of Archaeological Survey of India.

The style of Mathura sculpture borrows from the indigenous Indian traditions of the Maurya and Sunga periods. It displays a robust quality, full of life and vitality. The earliest abstract, geometric patterns were given up; and a more realistic touch was given to the sculptures. Static postures were replaced by figures that display a variety of movements and positions. It is based on a closer observation of life, although it is felt that the sculptures were based on the conceptual understanding of an object by an artist. There was a basic sense of idealism built into the sculptures. This is expressed by Ananda Coomarswamy in the following words:

> In Indian art it is not the appearance, but the significance of objects, human or otherwise, that is sought for ...In an abstract art, it is not the object, but a concept that stands before us. Majority of Mathura sculptures are religious in character. But the creativity of the artist is expressed in full, even though there are iconographical limitations in creating such sculptures.

The material used by the Mathura sculptor was reddish sandstone, sometimes spotted, from the local Sikri quaries. The reliefs in the sculptures are deeply cut; and the projecting and receding areas are very strongly highlighted. The most important focus of the sculptor is the human body. The figures wear minimum garments; and mostly the clothing they wear are transparent, giving an impression of nudity. The female figures are voluptuous and male figures are plump, indicating a sign of prosperity of that age. The faces as well as the limbs of these figures are fleshy. The heads of many of the statues are, of course, missing. Besides, most of these figures are adorned with jewellery and ornaments. This indicates two distinct features, namely that the society was those days prosperous; and that figures were of people of higher social status. Jewellery always symbolized a superior position in the society. Although Buddhist representations were more common among the sculptures, there were also representations belonging to Jain, and Brahmanical faiths. Some of the Buddhistic figures were free-standing images of the Buddha and Bodhisattvas. A second category of such figures stood as part of the ornamentation of monuments. The images of Buddha were in deep relief, giving the impression of sculptures in the round. The freestanding Bodhisattva figures are of a wide variety. The architectural fragments are normally part of stupas, pillars, gates(torana), tympana columns and capitals. The Mathura sculptors were fond of creating figures of semi-divine figures like yakshas, nagas, and *salabhanjika*. This is a tradition of worship of nature spirits, water spirits and tree spirits. One can view this as a continuation of the worship of forces of nature. These sculptures are of various postures. The voluptuous maidens of *salabhanjika* are indicative of importance given to fertility; and mother goddess. The pot bellied yakshas stand for abundance of wealth, and need for its protection. Flora, fauna and birds are also abundantly represented in the sculptures. The lion seems to be a very common animal, since it was representative of Sakya clan, and also denoted strength. The association of tree with women stood for the fecundity of nature.

The bachhanalian forms stand out as a distinctive category. The figure of the drunken courtesan with attendants excavated in Maholi, and the figures of Kubera drinking wine are representations of drinking and merry making. But they were presented in the context of Buddhist monuments. Art is also a representation of the social mores in the context of which it has flourished. No art stands out away from the customs and practices of the society. Looked at from that angle, we can decipher that the Buddhist traditions, and the religious practices were no doubt strong. At the same time, there was material prosperity in the society ruled by Kushanas because of vigorous trade and commerce. So enjoyment of life was widely accepted in terms of drinking, merry making and sensual pleasures.

Since such figures appear within the overall context of Buddhistic faith, it can be interpreted that the depiction of scenes of wine drinking was not a glorification of such activities, but rather a reminder that such practices are highly temporary and perishable as against the permanent verities taught through the Buddhistic and other religious orders.

Although stone was the predominant medium of Mathura sculptures, there are also figures of ivory, metal and terracota. Fragments of ivory boxes and ivory pieces of furniture decoration have been stored in Kabul Museum in Afghanistan. A bronze figure of Skanda was excavated from Sonkh. It is a beautiful figure indicating strength and virility. Terracota figures were also abundantly made. Terracota was often referred to as the art of the poor man, since these figures were made with the appeal to common man in mind. These were basically of two types, solid and hollow. The most common theme of terracota figures was the mother goddess, a symbol of fecundity; having the characterstic features of large breasts; slim waist and ample hips. Some figures represented both male and female with erotic overtones.

Mathura was the centre of Hindu Vasudeva cult, being the birthplace of Lord Krishna. During Kushana period quite a large number of Brahamanical figures were made, but they were substantially less in number than the number of Buddhist figures. But figures of Vishnu, Siva, Indra, Balarama and Surya formed an important part of the iconography of that period. There were representations of various aspects of the mother goddess, Laxmi, Durga and Saraswati. The revival of Hinduism, however, took place during the Gupta period. There are Jaina images also consisting of Tirthankara heads, and votive tablets. Two Jaina stupas were excavated from Kankali Tila. The Jaina images were quite similar to Buddhistic representations. During some periods of Indian history, Jainism had dominated over Buddhism; and it is surmised that in the first century BC the Jaina population outnumbered the Buddhist population.

The Gandhara School of Sculptures

The Gandhara school of sculpture flourished in the Northwest part of the Kushana empire - at present in Pakistan and Afghanistan. Peshawar, the ancient Purushapura was a main centre, being a capital city of the Kushanas. Another major centre was Taxila which was a later capital. The Gandharan cities were located on the important trade routes existing between China, Central Asia and the Mediterranean world. Gandhara became a melting pot of various cultures. Before Kushana rule was established over Gandhara in the 1st century AD, this territory was subjected to various rules like Mauryan rule (fourth-third century BC), Indo-Greek rule in Bactria (third-second century BC), and Sytho - Parthian domination (first century BC/1st century AD).

The artistic traditions of the Gandhara school bear a strong Hellenistic influence. The roots of this tradition are traced to the highly advanced civilization of Bactria which again was dominated by Hellenistic world. The high point of Gandhara school was reached during the first three centuries of the Christian era. The stone sculptures developed during this period; however the stucco, terracota and metal sculpture traditions continued well into the Gupta and post Gupta period. The main theme of sculpture was again Buddhistic. Buddhism had gone beyond the localized tradition of the Gangetic plains, whereas Jainism and Hinduism remained localized traditions around Mathura. During the reign of Kanishka, Buddhism flourished in the North.

The Gandhara sculptures are based on Greco-Roman school of art. The physical beauty of the human figure was captured in the sculptures. It leaned more towards "Realism" than the Mathura school. Greek and Roman art was the model. So spiritual and expressive qualities of these figures are less, since the predominant objective of the sculpture was to portray the beauty of the human body.

Stanislaw Czuma who made an in-depth study of the Gandhara sculptures has expressed the opinion that these sculptures contained a distinctive individual style in spite of the fact that many scholars considered these sculptures as merely a provincialised version of the Greco-Roman school of art. It was an eclectic form, but innovative in its own right. The figures were basically based on Hellenestic models. But the voluminous drapery with its intricate system of folds in raised ridges, rather than incised lines, particularly in the representation of Buddha images, seems to derive from the 'toga' of imperial Roman portraits. Most of the Gandhara sculptures are images of the Buddha and Bodhisattva. There are also architectural fragments and decorations, and bas-reliefs from the life of the Buddha. Most of the depictions are from the life of Buddha. It is also noticed that in the Gandhara school of architecture, the animal representations are less than in the Mathura school; floral motifs are of course common.

The material used by the Gandhara artist is a soft schist stone that varies in colour from lighter to darker gray. In some cases the stone was covered with gold leaf to make it look lustrous in dark. Stucco and terra cotta, being plentiful, inexpensive, represent, next to schist, the most popular media used by the Gandhara artist. Metal sculptures were rarer, and the majority of the bronzes dated to the period between the fifth and the seventh centuries AD, reflecting Gupta influence.

Bodhisattva of Maholi

This Bodhisattva figure is dated to 2nd century AD. It is sculpted out of red sandstone. The size of the figure is 167.5 x 76.5 x 29 cm, and is preserved in the National Museum, New Delhi.

The head, and both arms of this figures are missing. But the figure is sensuous, and it is a life size image. It shows a marked affinity to the Bodhisattva of the third year of Kanishka from Sarnath as well as to the one from Saheth - Maheth, the site of the ancient city of

Sravasti. It can thus be inferred that his right hand would have been raised towards the right shoulder, while the left would have rested on his hip. His flexed body with both feet firmly planted is in a strictly frontal attitude. The upper porlion of the body is bare except for a torque and flat multi-strand necklace, which is typical of Bodhisattvas. The lower portion is covered with a garment that clings to his body and is discernible at his loins and below the left knee. His garment is secured at the waist by a broad, double, flat belt; the upperstrand is knotted and falls over the right thigh. The ample folds of his garments hand down between his legs. The scarf that formed his upper garment probably, covered his left shoulder, in the extant remains it falls on his left thigh forming pleats which pass below his right knee.

The significance of the Bodhisattva figure is very high in the Buddhist religion. Such figures were produced in great numbers. Bodhisattva is one who attains enlightenment, but delays his own entry into bliss or nirvana in order to help others in the world to achieve enlightenment.

Kubera

This is a sculpture in red sandstone excavated from Ahichchatra in Bareilly District of Uttar Pradesh. This belongs to the period 2nd century AD corresponding to Kushana dynasty. 'Kubera' literally means a deformed figure. He is supposed to be the brother of Ravana in mythological literature, and is the guardian of the North besides being the god of wealth. The basic characterstics of the sculpture are elaborate treatment of the curled locks of hair, fully grown moustache which is tilted upwards at both ends and half-closed be mused eyes caused by consumption of intoxicating drinks. The lips are thick, and there is a pot belly. The limbs are short and the figure is dwarfish. The visible ornament is a thick necklace of twisted bands of pearls. The 'Yaksha' is supremely careless about his own figure, and reflects a zest for life, as well as a craving for enjoyment. This sculpture is displayed in National Museum, New Delhi.

Kubera is the leader of the Yaksas, one of the nature spirits that were worshipped as titular divinities as a part of the animistic pre-Aryan traditions. The Yakshas were believed to possess supernatural powers over wealth, fertility, illness-being capable of both benevolent and malevolent activities. Their worship was incorporated from popular folklore into the major religious systems, and it flourished under the Kusanas. Yakshas are secondary deities. They appear as attendants or guardians along with the main divine figures. But occasionally they also appear as independent idols, just as the figure of Kubera, who is a principal Yaksha.

The figure of Kubera is a dwarf with a potbelly. The treatment of the figure is humorous. The navel on the protruding belly is prominent. The lower garment or dhoti that the figure is supposed to be wearing has slipped below the navel and is invisible except for a few pleats behind his feet: His large, round head with ringlets carefully arranged in rows and his ample paunch stress the humorous aspects of this divine figure. While bringing out the caricatural qualities, the sculptor also has made this figure in such a manner that the viewer would get feelings of affection for their divinity. It is also surmised that the missing arms were probably raised upward in a gesture of support, and when the arms were broken off they damaged the ears of the figure, against which they would have rested.

The association of this figure with wine drinking is highly significant. It is an Indian equivalent of the

Hellenistic Dionysos or the Romas Bacchus, the patron of worldly pleasures. Like Bacchus, Kubera is often depicted as an obese drinker with a large belly. Kubera is associated with scenes of bacchanalian character. It is important to recollect here that in the Hindu mythology, wine - drinking was not banned in the world of divinity. The demi - gods in heaven; 'Devas' used to consume' somarasa' which is a type of wine of high quality. The 'Devas' did not have to possess austere qualities. They did indulge in the worldly pleasures. Obviously, Kubera, who is a yaksha and could be ranked among the demi-gods possessing divine powers, and yet not opposed to the pleasures of the senses, has been shown as a character in bacchanalian scenes. Since he is the guardian of wealth, he obviously would have the liberty of drinking wine, and would not refrain from such enjoyments which are commonly associated with the possession of wealth.

What, however, I nave observed in his intoxicated face, and bemused eyes is a certain kind of joviality, and a demeanour of carefreeness which one would not associate with an ordinary man of riches. A person possessing riches, but at the same time having great attachment to that would not be portrayed like this. The expression on the face of Kubera in the sculpture looks majestic, at the same time detached. It seems he is in the midst of his wealth and wine; and yet he has a deep realization of the temporary, ephemeral quality of worldly possession. As the divine guardian of wealth, he is very much dressed like one, but it seems that deep inside he is aware of the fleeting character of wealth. That is why, he does not look serious; he looks jovial and humorous. His squatting posture with protruding belly indicates the nature of his work as the guardian of wealth and guardian of the North, which in modem parlance can be described as sedentary.

Obviously, Kubera is carefree, and does not believe in watching his figure, in the process acquiring a pot belly. In the Indian lore, wealth is 'Chanchala', which means fast moving. That means wealth can never be rooted to one place. It has to move with speed. That is the basic nature of wealth. As the divine watchman of wealth, 'Kubera' could not be unaware of its basic nature. So he has looked at himself and the world in such a humorous and jovial manner. These are, however, interpretations which may be agreed to by many; and there will also be many having difference with such interpretation. One thing, however, is universally admitted. The sculpture of Kubera is a masterpiece of all times. This is a fine specimen of Mathura sculpture recovered from Ahichchatra. There have been more sculpture from Ahichhatra also giving rise to speculation that there was a local studio functioning there. The discussion about the sculpture of Kubera can be aptly summed up in the following words of Stanislaw Czuma.

"The Kubera from Ahichchatra represents not only technical excellence but is the powerful, expressive and humorous statement of a very talented artist."

Bachhanalian Relief with Intoxicated Courtesan and Vasantasena

This red sand stone sculpture of Maholi belonging to Mathura school is preserved in the National Museum, Delhi. This is a late 2nd century AD figure.

This is a double-faced relief, and belongs to the category of bachchanalian figures. Artistically, it is the most accomplished figure in this, group. This was excavated in Maholi village in the year 1938, along with the famous Bodhisattva figure from the ruins of Khanda vihara. These Bachchanalian images were set in the context of Buddhist monuments.

This is a magnificent double-sized relief. On one side is a bachchanalian (*Madhupana*) scene depicting a young and beautiful damsel, probably a courtesan, highly drunk in half-kneeling postures. She is supported by a tall, handsome male figure, most likely her lover on her right side. Her left hand rests on the shoulder of a Kubuja girl who holds a goblet in her hand. Opposite to the youth stands an old woman (*kultini*) looking at her mistress with great sorrow. V.S. Agrawal has, however, identified her as a hermaphrodite because of her undeveloped breasts, masculine shoulders and hips. It is well known that such attendants were being employed in royal harems. Over the head of the courtesan is shown a tree trunk with foliage supporting a partly visible bowl to highlight the environmental setting.

The depiction of this sensuous as well as erotic scene in the overall context. of Buddhist art appears intriguing to begin with. Such bachchanalian scenes are opposed to Buddhist values. But they might be intended to remind devotees of the pitfalls of pursuing sensual pleasures, and also indicate their impermanence, opposed to the permanent ideals preached by the Buddha. On the other hand, Buddhism preaches the middle path in which it was always possible to have the usual pleasures of the world. It also appears that such scenes are commonly depicted in Mathura school of art. The Indian artists were very much familiar with such drinking scenes, which originated from secular sources. Whatever be the way these scenes are interpreted against the religious ethos of Buddhism, it can be safely concluded that such depictions were firmly rooted in the traditions of Indian art. Art in many ways is a reflection of the society, and its practices and values. Therefore, this form of art proclaims that the society in ancient India was not prudish and epicurean values found a strong place in the social mores. Lets us for a moment think about the philosophy of 'Charbak' who preached that life has to be well lived, since after the end of it there is no return to the world. In the mainstream Hindu philosophy which preached the value of sacrifice, and renunciation, and also rebirth, and the recurring results of Karma which have to be gone through, this was certainly a deviant. But still it existed, and this school of thought could not be dismissed as something which was hopelessly marginal or peripheral. The existence of bachchanalian scenes in Buddhist settings may be interpreted as a reminder of impermanence of material pleasures; but it may not be necessarily so. In fact, such scenes were always popular with the ordinary temple goers. This means the scenes reflected a very strong and real part of social practices as they existed. It may, therefore, be realistic to accept them as they are; depictions and portrayals of actual happenings, and also certain pursuits of pleasure that society very commonly fancied despite the strong moral preachings of the religion, in this case, of Buddhism.

The bachhanalian figure being described is most beautifully executed. The hands of the intoxicated courtesan lie limp and lifeless. The other figures in the scene look like either helpless or distressed persons who are trying to support the beautiful courtesan who obviously has lost all sense of here and now. By all standards, it is a most beautiful sculpture.

On the reverse side of the relief is probably depicted a scene from the *Mrichchakatika* (The little clay cart), written by Sudraka. The story moves around 'Vasantasena', the most beautiful courtesan of Ujjain. Sakar, the brother-in-law of the king of Ujjain was in love with her, while she had inclination for someone else. One night she attended by her maid was followed by Sakar and his friend Vita on her way. Vita however, took pity on her and advised her to remove floral wreaths and anklets to hide her identity and escape. Vasantasena is shown in the sculpture as removing the garlands and also pushing her anklets to her knees, so that she would not be recognized as the courtesan, and could then manage to run from the designs of Sakara. The cowardly Sakara is shown as hiding behind Vita. Vasantasena is attended by a maid holding an umbrella.

The Vasantasena relief is again a great masterpiece of Mathura art. The relief is deep, and a three-dimensional impression is created. Great fluidity of rhythm and motion has been reflected by showing different poses and gestures of the figures. The figures are sensitively handled suiting to the requirements of the story.

Stanislaw Czuma has interpreted that the Vasantasena sculpture contrasts with bachchanalian scene on the other side, just as virtue would oppose vice. The drinking scene is the story of a weak courtesan falling to the vice of drinking. Vasantasena, however, being no ordinary courtesan runs away from the evil eyes of Sakara since she is faithful to someone else.

The sensuous figures on this relief are very prominently visible in the background of Buddhist monuments. Otherwise also voluptuous yakshis are depicted on the railings and pillars of stupas. What does it signify as against the monastic order of Buddhist monks? It most likely indicates the presence of wordly attachments of which the devotee is to be aware. On the other hand, it also shows that there was a sensuous stream existing in the society of those times, while Buddhist order preached the middle path, which meant that in order to pursue the truth, the seeker has to give up wordly pleasures, at least in a substantial measure. It is to be remembered in this context that erotic sculptures adorned the walls of many a Hindu temple also, surprising and shocking many western commentators. But most likely, the message there was also the same; That sensual attractions are a fact of life; and one has to be careful about their strong presence, in order to finally overcome them, and pursue the path of the Divine.

Buddhist Tympanum (Torana)

This is a fragmentary archway (*torana*) representing half of a tympanum carved on both sides. It had once formed part of the gateway to a stupa. This is an important part of Buddhist architecture. The sculpture is kept in the National Museum in Delhi. It is made of spotted red sand stone, and is of the size 95.5 x 80 x 115 cm. It was discovered in Jamalpur, Mathura in 1st century AD. In this connection it is mentioned that the use of archway leading to a Buddhist edifice was introduced into Mathura from Gandhara.

The design of the slab is as follows. The entire slab on both faces is divided into three registers by concentric arches. On the obverse, at the centre of the three registers, several figures have been depicted. From top to bottom, one is presented with an alms - bowl filled with offerings; Buddha seated on Padmasana, in 'Abhayamudra'. On the reverse, the three registers reveal several figures. At the centre of the top register the Buddha's headdress is presented. In the middle register, the Bodhisattva Maitreya is seated on Padmasana with a prominent wheel symbol (Chakra) on the soles of his upturned feet (*Vajraparyankasana*). He displays the gesture of assurance (*Abhayamudra*) with his right hand while he holds a flask with his left. In the lowest register, only the fragment of a scalloped hallow is extant. The comer spaces are decorated on both sides with formalized eagles (Garuda) below which in each register, are represented open-mouthed crocodile-like creatures with sharp teeth. The worshippers depicted on both sides are flying celestials. These figures carry baskets of flowers in the left hands while showering petals from the flowers with their right hands.

The Jamalpur archway dates from the transition stage when the Mathura school changed from the Hinayana to the Mahayana form of Buddhism.

Another such tympanum made of red sand stone (ht. 76 cm, Wth. 55 em) belonging to the same period, i.e. 1 st century AD is kept in the Museum of Fine Arts, Boston. This is half of a tympanum originally placed above the doorway leading to a Buddhist edifice. It is arch-shaped with a lotus bud suspended from the centre of the arch. A relief decorates both sides each one comprising two scenes placed within two tiers, narrowing at the sides, and forming a crescent with floral bands separating the tiers.

The relief belongs to the early ani-conic phase of Kusana art, wher Buddha was not yet depicted in anthropomorphic form, but only referred to in terms of symbols. This was the Hinayana period of Buddhism. The obverse of the relief has in the lower register a *caityavrksha* (or bodhi tree) with a railing round it. Above it, in the upper register, is the throne with begging bowl of Buddha, a greatly venerated relic with a scalloped halo surrounding it.

The reverse side is decorated in the lower section with a religious edifice, or chaitya; above it, in the top register is a cosmic pillar with the *dharmachakra*. Each emblem is flanked by lotuses and curtains that often frame venerated objects. A variety of worshippers flank each of the centralized symbols. There are animal figures like deer, monkey, tiger and lion. There are figures combining the body parts of human beings and animals. The comers of the tympanum are decorated with the sculptures of the mythical bird, Garuda holding a snake in its beak.

It may be noted that in the tympanum of Jamalpur there are Buddha and Bodhisattva figures. But in the tympanum kept in the Museum of Fine Arts, Boston there are no human figures of Buddha and Bodhisattva. That being the difference, there are many similarities. This also indicates a period of transition from the aniconic phase to the anthropomorphic phase. The Hinayana period of Buddhism was yielding place to the Mahayana period of Buddhism. The Jamalpur tympanum refers to the early Kanishka period, whereas the other tympanum refers to pre-Kanishka period.

These decorated archways to stupas also contain many motifs, which are associated with Hindu worship. For example Garuda is the divine bird in Hindu mythology, being considered as the Vahana of Lord Vishnu. The philosophy of decorating the archway to the place of worship by religious motifs is to prepare the mind for a spirit of devotion. This is common to both Buddhist and Hindu places of worships. Normally, *toranas* (archways), doors, gates, etc. are adorned with semi divine figures, and important religious motifs and symbols are supposed to prepare the devotee's mind for a higher devotional level in which he can worship the main deity.

Standing Buddha (Gandhara) Kushana 2nd Century ad

This sculpture of size 112 x 39 x17 cm is kept in the National Museum, New Delhi. This is a magnificent specimen of Gandhara art of the Peshawar Valley. This is sculpted out of dark grey schist. This is a most captivating figure of Sakyamuni. This represents typical

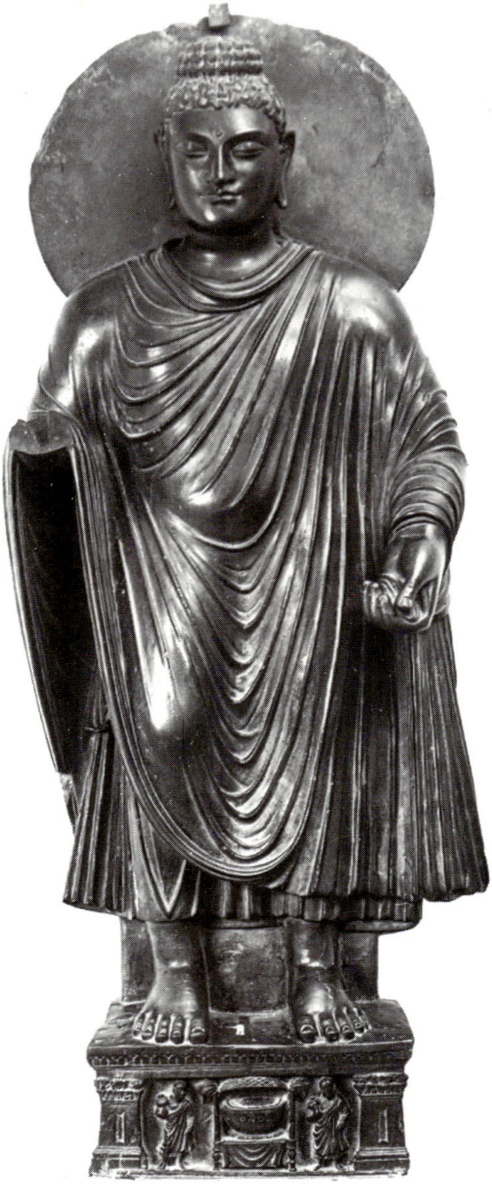

Buddha, Kushana, 2nd Cent. A. D., Gandhara, Schist

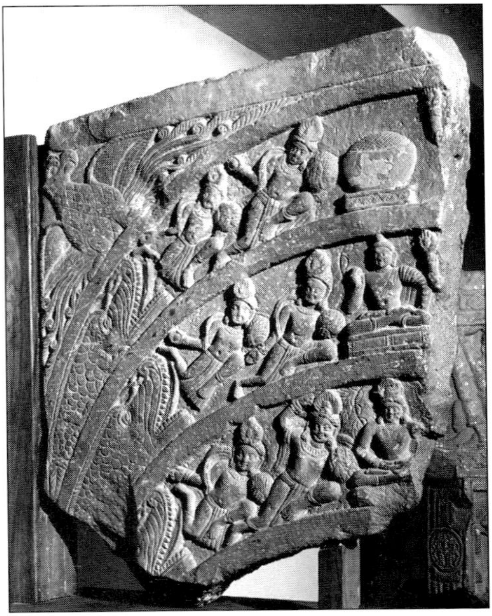

Buddhist Tympanum(*torana*) Kushana, 1st Cent. A. D., Jamalpur, Mathura

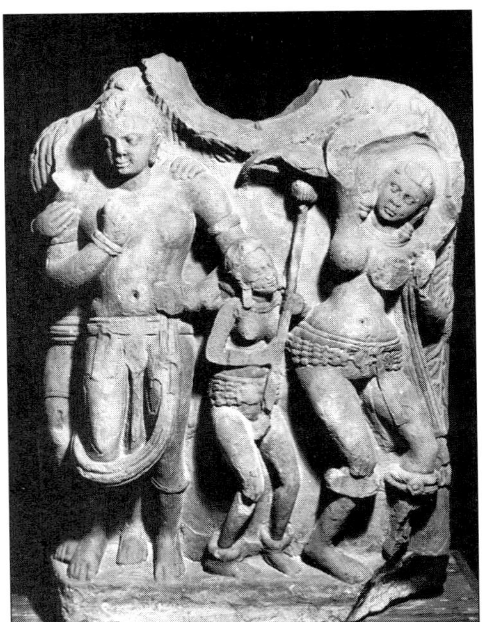

Bacchanalian Scene, Kushana, 2nd Cent. A.D. Maholi, Mathura

4

Two Islamic Monuments in Delhi and Agra

PART I
HUMAYUN'S TOMB

Introduction

The arrival of Muslim rule in India marked a new phase of customs and practices and a new architectural style. The defeat of the Rajput ruler, Prithviraja Chauhana in the battle of Tarai by Muhammad bin Sam of Ghur in 1192 AD saw the beginning of rule of Sultans in Delhi. After the victory, Muhammad left the reign under the control of his slave, Qutbu'd-Din' Aibak who was the first ruler of the Slave dynasty in Delhi. Qutbu'd-Din established himself as the ruler of Delhi after the death of Muhammad in 1206 AD.

The establishment of the Slave dynasty saw the emergence of a continuous rule of nearly seven centuries by the Muslim rulers under various dynasties. The various dynasties which ruled in India with Delhi as capital are as follows:

1. Slave or Mamluk dynasty, including Balban and his successors — 1206-1290 AD

2.	Khalji dynasty	1290-1321 AD
3.	Tughloq dynasty	1321-1414 AD
4.	Sayyid dynasty	1414-1444 AD
5.	Lodi dynasty	1452-1526 AD
6.	Sur dynasty	1540-1555 AD

The last of the Lodi rulers, Ibrahim Lodi (1517-26 AD) during the end of his rule became suspicious and started ill treating his nobles and even provincial governors. Due to this a sense of resentment prevailed among the various noble men of his time. The governor of Lahore, Daulat Khan who was troubled by the Delhi Sultan, invited Babur to attack Ibrahim Lodi. Babur met Ibrahim Lodi in the famous first battle of Panipat in 1526 AD. Ibrahim Lodi was defeated and killed in the battle and Babur became the ruler of Delhi and a large tract of north India which was under the control of Lodis. Babur established the great Mughal dynasty, the famous rulers of which are mentioned below:

Mughal dynasty (1526-1857 AD).

(a) Babur (1526-1530 AD)

(b) Humayun (1530-40; 1555-56 AD)

(c) Akbar (1556-1605 AD)

(d) Jahangir (1605-1627 AD)

(e) Shah Jahan (1627-1658 AD)

(f) Aurangazeb (1658-1707 AD)

(g) Later Mughals (1707-1857 AD)

The Imperial character of the Mughals ended with the death of Aurangazeb in 1707 AD although the later Mughals carried on the rule with much diminished vigour until 1857 when the British government formalised their rule in India.

After capturing Delhi, Babur sent his son Humayun to take control of Agra. Babur established gardens at

Agra and Panipat, the one at Agra known as Aram Bagh, now corrupted as Ram Bagh. He established a new pattern of terrace gardens in India, the idea of which originated in the mountainous and slopy terrains of Kabul area. During his short reign he defeated many of the regional kingdoms of north India and gained control of a vast territory which formed as a solid platform for his successors. Babur was also a great builder and he mentions in his Memoirs about his various endeavours. Some of the buildings either built directly by him or under his patronage are Kabuli Bagh mosque at Panipat, the Jami'-Masjid at Sambhal, and a mosque at Ayodhya.

Humayun succeeded Babur in 1530 AD soon to face resistance from the hands of Sher Shah, descendant of Ibrahim Khan, an Afghan from Sur. Humayun was defeated and driven out of Delhi in 1540. Humayun took shelter in Iran and witnessed a series of hardships for nearly 15 years in exile during which period his son Akbar also was born. Humayun returned ultimately with a borrowed Persian army in 1555 AD and defeated Sikandar Shah Sur, the son and successor of Sher Shah Sur.

However, he died soon in 1556 AD falling from his library stairs. The reign of Humayun was short and he did not concentrate on consolidating the territory he inherited from his father. During this short reign he made some ventures in building activity. In 1533 AD he laid the foundations of Dinpanah, a new city on the right bank of the river Yamuna. This fort was completed within a short period of ten months; the building material largely came from the spoiled material from the Siri Fort. The remains of Dinpanah are not traceable now, as it was largely modified and destroyed by Sher Shah. Humanyun also completed the partly built Purana Qila by Sher Shah. He was also instrumental for construction of buildings like Jamali-Kamali masjid in Mehrauli, Delhi, mosque in Kachhpura, Agra, etc. Humayun used the Sher Mandal in Purana Qila as his library, from where he slipped, fell down and died in 1556 AD.

The construction of the mausoleum of Humayun was commenced by his senior widow, known as.Haji Begum in 1565 AD, nine years after Humayun's death.

Characteristics of Indo-Islamic Architecture

The Islamic rule in India saw the introduction of many new elements in the building style. This was very much distinct from the already prevailing building style adopted in the construction of temples and other secular architecture. The main element in the Islamic architecture is the introduction of arches and domes, and it is the arcuate style of construction while the traditional Indian building style is trabeate, using pillars and beams and lintels. The early buildings of the Slave dynasty did not employ true Islamic building styles and consisted of false domes and false arches. Later, the introduction of true arches and true domes started to appear; the earliest example is the Alai Darwaza by the side of Qutb Minar.

The different religious beliefs are also reflected in the mode of construction and architectural styles. The Islamic style also incorporated many elements from the traditional Indian style and a compound style emanated. The introduction of decorative brackets, balconies, pendentive decorations, etc in the architecture is an example in this regard. The other distinguishing features of Indo Islamic architecture are the utilisation of kiosks *(chhatris)*, tall towers *(minars)* and half-domed double portals. As human worship and its representation are not allowed in Islam, the buildings and other edifices are generally decorated richly in geometrical and arabesque designs. These designs were carved on stone in low relief, cut on plaster, painted or inlaid. The use of lime as mortar was also a major element distinct from the traditional building style.

The tomb architecture is also another feature of the Islamic architecture as the practice of the burial of the dead is adopted. The general pattern of the tomb architecture consisted of a domed chamber *(hujra)*, a cenotaph in its centre with a *mihrab* on the western wall and the real grave in the underground chamber. To this general tomb architecture, the Mughals added a new dimension by introducing gardens all around the tomb. The Mughal tombs are generally placed at the centre of a huge garden complex, the latter being sub-divided into square compartments, the style being known as *char-bagh*. The Mughals also built large gardens in various levels and terraces on the *char-bagh* pattern. Scholars trace the evolution of the *char-bagh* pattern of gardening to the original land of the Mughals, the Kabul Valley, where depending upon the landscape and terrain, gardens and residential complexes were laid out. The Mughals inherited this garden type and superbly transformed it according to the new terrains in India. Thus, evolved a transformed style of *char-bagh* pattern of gardening.

The Mughals are also credited to have introduced the double dome system of dome architecture and the *pietra-dura* style of inlay decorations.

The Tomb Complex

There are various views regarding internment of the body of Humayun. It is generally agreed that his body was initially buried in the Purana Oila, later moved to a temporary burial tomb in Sirhind, due to the invasion of Hemu in 1556. His body was again brought back to

Delhi and buried in the Sher Mandal when Akbar defeated Hemu, and ultimately to the present location when the mausoleum was built by his begum and widow, Haji Begum in 1569. The mausoleum was built at an estimated cost of rupees fifteen lakhs. The Humayun's tomb marks the beginning of the major building activities of the Mughals.

The building style is a combination of Persian architecture and indigenous building styles. The right combination of the red sandstone building medium with the white marble, the latter used as large inlays, exhibits the maturity of this style. This kind of combination of red sandstone and white marble in the tombs could be invariably seen in the architecture of Delhi Sultanates of 14th century AD. The earliest example, of course, is the Alai Darwaza which has exquisite white marble decorations over red sandstone background. The Mughals readopted this style of decorative architecture and in a sense revived this technique of construction. The other buildings which used this style of decoration include the mosque of Jamali Kamali (ca. 1528-29), the Qala-i-Kuhna mosque (ca. 1534) and the tomb of Ataga Khan (ca. 1556-67).

The Humayun tomb is located at the centre of a huge garden complex. The garden complex is divided mainly into four compartment further being sub-divided into many square parts (a typical example of Mughal *char-bagh)*, with causeways and water channels, and water pavilions at regular intervals. The tomb complex is enclosed by a high rubble wall; with entrance gateways, one on the west and other on the south, the latter being closed now. The south gate rises to a height of nearly 15.5 metres and consists of a central octagonal hall flanked by rectangular rooms. The first floor of the gateway has square and oblong rooms. On the outside, the gate is flanked by screen-walls with arched recesses. Immediately to the west of the south gateway is an enclosure measuring 146 metres by 32 metres, built against the exterior face of the enclosure wall. The building is a low-roofed one with 25 arched entrances and was meant to house the attendants of the royal tomb. Another building is also located nearby, which along with the above enclosure is a later addition. At present, the western gate is used by the visitors to enter the tomb complex. The west gate is smaller in comparison to the south gate and rises to a height of 7 metres and is also double-storeyed.

The northern, southern and western walls of the boundary wall are built of rubble stone and its interior face consists of recessed arches. On the eastern side, the height of the enclosure wall is subdued and was originally meant as an access to the Yamuna river which is flowing nearby.

The tomb proper is constructed over a huge elevated platform 6.5 m in height, the face of which is relieved by a series of arched openings on all four sides, except four entrance stairs, one each at the centre of four sides. There are 17 arched openings on each of the four sides, and the corners are chamfered. The combination of the arched openings and the chamfered corners gives an aesthetic look to the whole monument.

The building medium in the Humayun's Tomb is of three kinds of stones, viz., red sandstone, while marble and quartzite. The enclosure walls and the two gateways are constructed of local quartzite with red sandstone dressing and marble inlay. The stairs of platform of the main tomb is also dressed with quartzite. The quartzite is locally available in the ridges of Delhi, while the red sandstone came from the mines of Tantpur near Agra and white marble from the famous Makrana mines of Rajasthan.

The ascending stairs at the centre of each of the four sides of the elevated platform leads to an open terrace, at the centre of which is located the main tomb. The main tomb is located below the monument and is approached through a horizontal passage to the east of southern stair. The arched openings of the platform contain many miscellaneous tombs.

The main tomb is octagonal on plan and rises into two storeys; at the four diagonal corners of the octagon are four chambers, which also house many tombs of the family members of Humayun. The octagonal tomb is surmounted by a double dome supported by squinches. The employment of double dome in a mausoleum is first seen here and this gives the builder the advantage of building an imposing structure of enormous height, tactfully concealing the presence of double domes on the outside. While the exterior height gives an imposing look, the low ceiling of the lower dome gives a proportionate height of the interior features. The pattern of constructing double domes was already prevalent in West Asia during this period which was first introduced in the Humayun's tomb.

The dome of this mausoleum is also a complete one, in the sense that it makes a full circle when completed on the other side too. The outline of the dome represents a complete semi-circle and thus a distinct variation from the earlier varieties of the dome architecture. The main mausoleum, as mentioned above, rises in two storeys and could be viewed in three stages. The lower one consists of eight arched openings of the octagon, above which is a balconied arch opening, over which is the intrados of the inner dome, decorated with red sandstone jallies. The interior face of the main tomb is also relieved with different kinds of stone and the white marble as the bordering inlay decorative patterns. The red sandstone jali decorations could be seen at the mid arched openings placed at its lower level.

The extrados of the mausoleum is veneered with white marble stones in contrast to the largely red sandstone building. The dome is bulbous in shape; the skyline is relieved with small pavilions on the four corners along side the main dome.

The Humayun's Tomb is also associated with the tragic capture of the last of the Mughal Emperors, Bahadur Shah Zafar, along with the three princes Mirza Mughal, Mirza Khizar Sultan and Mirza Abu Bakr by Lieutenant Hudson in 1857. The Mughal Emperor along with the princes was captured by Hudson on 22 September, 1857.

The Humayun's Tomb complex also houses many other prominent buildings which are examples of architecture of the period preceding and succeeding Humayun. The prominent among them are:

Barber's Tomb

The tomb is located at the southeast corner in the garden complex. The tomb is datable to 1590-91, through an inscription found inside. The person interned in this tomb is unknown, the local name of the tomb is Barber's Tomb (Nai ka Gumbad).

Nila Gumbad

The monument is located outside the eastern enclosure wall, which is locally known as Nila Gumbad, due to the blue coloured~dome. It is believed to contain the remains of one Fahim Khan, the attendant of Abdur Rahim Khan, who lived during the reign of Jahangir. The attendant died in 1626 AD.

Chillah Nizamuddin Aulia

The building is located outside to the northeast corner of the mausoleum and is in Tughluq style. The building is believed to be the residence of Shaik Nizamuddin Aulia who died in 1325 AD.

Afsarwala Mosque

The mosque is located to the southwest of the west gate of the main mausoleum, the building is dated between 1560 and 1567 based on the architectural style.

Afsarwala Tomb

The tomb is located adjacent to the Afsarwala Mosque, and is an unidentified tomb. One of the marble graves inside the tomb has a date of 1566-67 AD.

Arab-ki-Sarai

The sarai was built by Haji Begum, the widow of Humayun in 1560-61 to house the three hundred Arab priests, who were said to have been brought with her from her pilgrimage to Mecca. Another version is that the building housed the Persian workers and craftsmen who were actually engaged in building the Humayun's Tomb. The sarai is located adjacent to the Afsarwala mosque.

Garden of Bu Halima

The visitor entering the Humayun Tomb complex first enters into a garden complex, known as the Bu Halima garden. However, the origin of the name is not known and the garden on its style could be datable to the early Mughals.

Tomb and Mosque of Isa Khan

The tomb and mosque of Isa Khan is located to the south of the Bu Halima garden. An inscription on a red sandstone slab indicated that the tomb is of Masnad Ali Isa Khan, son of Niyaz Aghwan, the Chief chamberlain, and was built during the reign of Islam Shah, son of Sher Shah, in 1547-48 AD.

PART II
I'TIMAD-UD-DAULA'S TOMB, AGRA

I'timad-ud-daula or the "Lord Treasurer" was the title given to Mirza Ghiyath Beg under the reign of Emperor Jahangir, who was the father-in-law of the emperor and father of Nurjahan. Mirza Ghiyath Beg was the son of Khwaja Muhammad Shariff, the Prime Minister of Khurasan. Mirza Ghiyath Beg came to India after the death of his father and was enrolled in the royal service by Akbar after being introduced to him. He was an able person and due to his merit he received several honours and slowly rose in the society. Initially, he was promoted to the *mansab* of 1000 horse and after his daughter married Jahangir, he was promoted to 2000 *zat* (personnel) and 500 *sawar* (horsemen). Later, he was made the *Vazir* of the Empire. His *mansab* was gradually rising, from 4000/1000 *(zat/sawar)* in 1612, 5000/2000 in 1614, 6000/3000 in 1615 with standard and drum, 7000/5000 in 1614 and ultimately to 7000/7000 in 1619. He died in 1622.

The beautiful mausoleum for her father, Mirza Ghiyath Beg or the I'timad-ud-daula was constructed by Nurjahan, the consort of Emperor Jahangir, between 1622 and 1628. The mausoleum is located on the left bank of river Yamuna and downstream to the Ram Bagh, Chini-ka-Rauza, other famous monuments on the left bank of the river.

The tomb complex represents the example of a typical Mughal *char-bagh* tomb pattern, with the main mausoleum placed at the centre of a huge garden complex, measuring 165 X 165 metres, enclosed on all sides by high walls, and entered through an impressive gateway on its east. On the river-side an equally impressive water pavilion with central chamber and side alleys is provided. The garden was irrigated through shallow water channels, the water supplied by two overhead water tanks located on the river-side.

The Main Mausoleum

As stated above, the main building medium of this mausoleum is white marble while the ancillary buildings are constructed of red sandstone. Other basic feature of the mausoleum is the excellent usage of inlay decorations. The use of marble as the main building material is a marked transition from the red sandstone buildings of the Akbar era to that of white marble buildings of Jahangir and Shah Jahan. Jahangir is known to have effectively made a beginning in the introduction of white marble as a building as well as a decorative medium in the architecture. This change in the building style was fully adopted by his son and successor, Shah Jahan in his buildings. Hence, the tomb of I'timad-ud-daula is an important example of the architecture of the period of transition.

The main mausoleum is square on plan and is built over a raised platform of red sandstone. The raised platform has four tanks with a central fountain on each of the sides, in front of the central arch of the main mausoleum. The main mausoleum is constructed of white marble, while the entrance gateways and other pavilions are of red sandstone with profuse white marble inlay decorations. The tomb, which is square on plan, is having octagonal towers on the four corners, which attain a circular plan after it surpasses the terrace and are crowned by *chhattries*.

Each face of the facade of the tomb is relieved by three arches, the central one serving the purpose of entrance and exit, while the flanking ones are closed beautifully with the help of ornamental *jalis* (trellis screens). Each *jali* is unique in the pattern of decoration with the aid of geometrical design patterns. The facade is given a sloping eave *(chhajja)* supported by carved brackets above the arched openings. Above the eave is a *jalied* balustrade. The *jalis*, whether on the facade or the balustrade are representations of excellent workmanship of trellis screen designs and are exquisitely executed. Some scholars are of the view that these actually are copies of ivory workmanship; such is the detail of the design pattern and the masterly way in which they are executed.

On plan, the tomb complex consists of a central square hall, with four rectangular chambers at the centre, one on each side and four square chambers, one each on the corner of the mausoleum. All these chambers are located all around the central chamber and are interconnected through passages. The central chamber contains the cenotaphs of Mirza Ghiyath Beg (I'timad-ud-daula) and Asmat Begum, the parents of Nurjahan. Some of the corner chambers contain tombstones of Ladli Begum (daughter of Nurjahan) and her husband Sher Afkun (popularly known as Sher Afghan).

The upper storey of the mausoleum is also a square chamber directly above the central chamber of the ground floor. The chamber of the upper storey is a *'barahdari'* with three arched openings on each side. The central openings of the north and southern sides are only open, while the remaining ones are closed with *jalis*. The *jalis* are again decorated with beautifully decorated geometrical designs. The facade is decorated with an overhanging *chhajja*. The chamber is crowned by a pyramidal roof and not by a conventional dome of the contemporary period buildings. The pyramidal roof is crowned by lotus-petal design pattern, which is again crowned by four *kalash* finials at the four angles. The other architectural feature of this building is the arrangement of the four circular corner towers, directly rising from the four corner octagonal towers of the ground floor. These corner towers rise elegantly and are arranged in symmetry with the central chamber.

Decorative Patterns of the Mausoleum

The tomb of I'timad-ud-daula is an excellent example of the exhibition of various decorative patterns and elements and styles of the contemporary period. The mausoleum is also an example of excellent *pietra dura* (inlay decoration) and is often considered to be a precursor of the similar decorative patterns at the Taj Mahal. The inlay decorations are executed on a white marble background with various coloured stones and paintings. The pattern of decoration consists of division of the surface of the tomb into several running bands with borders, and panels again which are bordered, both horizontal and vertical. The plinth of the mausoleum is decorated with bands of highly stylised floral pattern, the main pattern being a honeysuckle motif. This pattern is bordered with a continuous knob and flower pattern.

The wall area above the plinth and to a height of a normal waist height is divided into several dados, both on the exterior as well as interior. These dados are decorated with exquisite geometrical inlay patterns bordered by creepers and honeysuckle pattern. Above the dados are noticed ornamental decorative patterns in vertical bands, and they are bordered by ornamental cartouches. This pattern of decorative ornamentation is continued on all the sides up to the towers, up to the frieze and even below the *chhajja*.

Apart from the above decorative patterns, the other elements of designs are cups, wine-vases and *guldastas*, which are the distinctive decorative elements of the period of Jahangir. The other decorative motifs include that of five-petalled flower, cloud-form, plant compositions, arabesque and stylised florals, etc. These decorative patterns are decorated in abundance in inlaid mosaic on both sides of the entrance arches above the dado areas. The *guldasta* is a floral composition consisting of twigs, leaves and flowers emanating from a pot. The cypress motif, a typical Persian motif and a symbol of grief, is used on the inner side of the arches. The cups, vases and *guldastas* are used at various places including the corner towers. The decorative, patterns are in profusion covering each and every inch of the surface of the mausoleum. However, the profusion is not monotonous. The monotony is effectively broken by the usage of several decorative designs and mosaics, utilisation of different coloured stones, putting them into use in the several horizontal and vertical panels.

The pavilion on the upper storey is also decorated with similar inlay and mosaic patterns of the ground floor. The pavement of this chamber is excellently decorated with various motifs like that of five-petalled flower, honeysuckle, cloud-form, etc., in an arabesque designed one.

The stucco and painted decorative patterns are mostly seen on the interior chambers of the ground floor. These decorations are also executed in motifs like *guldastas,* wine-vase, cypress and other Persian motifs. The Chinese cloud-forms named as the 'tchi' are used excellently in the blank spaces in each panel and alcove. The ceiling decorations consist of stalactite patterns which are stylised designs in incised stucco, executed in deep blue, crimson and golden colours. The ceilings of northern and southern halls are noteworthy for the beautiful relief and incised stucco-work. The ceilings of the eastern and western halls have cartouches of incised stucco which resemble typical embroidery design patterns.

Apart from the geometrical and mosaic design patterns used as decorations in the mausoleum, animal motifs are also noticeable as a decorative motif. The animal motifs are mainly seen as painted decorations in the interior, mostly inside the jar-shaped *guldastas*. The most commonly depicted animal is the peacock. The other animals depicted are fish, rats, dogs, lions and mythical animals. The depiction of human figures in the decorations is a surprise element as such decorative motifs are uncommon in Islamic art. The human figures are seen as painted motifs, in the *guldasta* motif. Many of the *guldastas* contain a *chhattri* decoration, with a seated human figure inside it.

Some scholars are of the opinion that the inlay decoration which is noticed in profusion in various decorative patterns at this mausoleum is an indigenous development. They feel that the usage of white marble inlay in the red sandstone medium at the monuments like Humayun's Tomb and palaces of Red Fort, Agra might have served as precursors to such inlay decorations. In fact, the inlay decorations as a decorative medium can be traced as early as the Alai Darwaza of the Qutb Complex. Here too, white marble inlays are effectively used in the red sandstone medium. Thus, the inlay decorations of the later period marble monuments like the I'timad-ud-daula and the Taj Mahal are an indigenous development.

The I'timad-ud-daulah tomb stands as an excellent example of the inlay decorative art as well as of the transitory stage of Mughal architecture.

References

Archaeological Survey of India (2002), *Humayun's Tomb & Adjacent Monuments*, Delhi.

Brown, P. (1997), *Indian Architecture (Islamic Period)*, Taraporvala, Mumbai (rep.).

Ebba, Koch (2002), *Mughal Architecture*, Delhi.

Nath, R. (1982), *History of Mughal Architecture*, Vol. I, Delhi.

——(1997), *Agra and its Monuments*, Agra.

Sharma, Y. D. (1990), *Delhi and its Neighbourhood*, Delhi (rep.).